Piaget's theory

Piaget's theory

A psychological critique

Geoffrey Brown and **Charles Desforges**

Routledge & Kegan Paul · London, Boston and Henley

First published in 1979
by Routledge & Kegan Paul Ltd
39 Store Street, London WC1E 7DD,
Broadway House, Newtown Road,
Henley-on-Thames, Oxon RG9 2EN and
9 Park Street, Boston, Mass. 02108, USA

Set in IBM Journal by
Hope Services, Abingdon
and printed in Great Britain by
Redwood Burn Ltd, Trowbridge & Esher

British Library Cataloguing in Publication Data
Brown, Geoffrey, b. 1935
    Piaget's theory.
    1. Cognition in children   2. Piaget, Jean
    I. Title   II. Desforges, Charles
    155.4'13   BF723.C5   79-40870

ISBN 0 7100 0392 7

Contents

Chapter 1

Piaget and theories of development

As a prelude to evaluating Piaget's theory we raise some general issues about the problems of accounting for cognitive development, and contrast Piaget's stance on these issues with those adopted by other authorities.

Many of the differences between a newborn infant and a two-year-old child are obvious. The elder child is bigger, more mobile, less dependent, has a wide repertoire of physical skills, can communicate many of his needs, has tastes, opinions, attitudes, favourite people, remembers a range of facts, names, times and promises and responds in elaborate ways to approaches made to him by others. Despite his achievements, however, he is a social, emotional and intellectual novice when compared with a four-year-old. The theorist working in developmental psychology seeks to explain these dramatic, age related changes.

In this undertaking a number of perennial issues are met. If some account is to be given of the changes as development proceeds then it is necessary to have detailed and accurate descriptions of the achievements at certain reference points. This in turn entails making choices about which part of the child's extensive behavioural repertoire to describe since it is unlikely that any exhaustive description could be possible. Given these necessarily selective descriptions of developmental attainments the theorist then has to consider how development proceeds. Will the acquisition be seen as gradual accumulations of experience or as abruptly appearing achievements, and, as a related issue, are the attainments of the four-year-old *qualitatively* different from those of the two-year-old or are they simply *quantitatively* different? Is the four-year-old's language, for example, more of the same kind

1

of language that the two-year-old exhibits or is the elder child in possession of a radically different mode of communication? A fourth problem in accounting for development requires that the theorist explain the differential role of innate and experiential factors and of their possible interactions. How far is the child's mode and level of intellectual functioning biologically determined at conception? How do particular life experiences interact with biological factors to enhance or limit the production of behaviours?

These problems of describing and accounting for developmental change are inter-related in complex ways. The selections made will not be random. The theorist will observe those specific behaviours which are felt to be most related to the problem he has in mind, and the conception of the problem will be informed by his stance on the nature/nurture debate, or on whether he conceives development to be a gradual and continuous accumulation of behavioural elements or a discontinuous, stepwise process of emergent functions. Of course the reverse process of influence is also true. Not only does our conception of development inform the kinds of data we select to solve problems of theory, the subsequent descriptions of behaviour in turn constrain our view of how development proceeds.

Put bluntly, the conception of a problem necessarily informs the selection of the data chosen as pertinent to the problem and selective and limited data necessarily constrain the subsequent view of the problem. In what follows, this point will be illustrated again and again. Whether, in the process of building theories of development, the above describes a vicious circle of self confirmation or a growing spiral of understanding, we set aside for the moment.

The nature of theory

In common usage, the term 'theory' has a number of more or less vague connotations. It may imply a hunch, 'my theory is the butler did it' means that the story so far leads me to believe that the butler is the most likely culprit of some crime. Speculations less directly linked to facts are often termed 'theories'. We see a friend getting fatter and 'theorise' or 'speculate' or 'suspect' that they are anxious, because we know from past experience that this friend eats a lot when snowed under with work and we take this excess eating to be a consequence of anxiety. This dual role of summarising and accounting for facts is entailed in the word 'theory' both in its common sense and formal-scientific usage. Equally, common sense distinguishes between good and bad theory or speculation. Good speculation is, quite simply, speculation which 'comes true'. Scientific theory is similarly demanding. Good theory is theory from which accurate predictions and adequate explanations can be made. One final distinction made in common usage is between promising theory and unpromising theory. There are lines of argument or procedures for making predictions about winning on a fruit machine or betting on horses which, whilst in the short term are not producing satisfying outcomes, none the less look sufficiently worthwhile to polish, amend slightly or persevere with. That is, there are theories which, for more or less vague reasons, we go along with because we believe they can be improved. Scientists also recognise that new theories may be temporarily unsatisfactory in terms of predictive and explanatory capacity but if, for other reasons, the theory looks promising, then it may be subjected to rigorous procedures of amendment.

A scientific theory is a conceptual tool used to describe and predict efficiently, and explain adequately, a given set of phenomena. The set of phenomena may be extremely limited or highly complex. We can contrast, for example, the problem of describing the increase in children's height with age against that of describing the increase in intellectual competence with age. Height is readily conceptualised and can be represented by a single quantity on a single scale. But what constitutes 'intellectual competence' and how is it to be represented?

If describing a set of phenomena is daunting, the question of 'adequately explaining' the set is even more so since theorists must offer not only a definition and representation of the phenomena but also make those statements that allow the description to be tested as an explanation. In science such tests tend to require empirical work. Thus a scientific theory takes the form of a proposition or set of propositions from which empirically testable hypotheses can be deduced.

Some problems in building and evaluating scientific theories

A necessary preliminary to appraising a theory critically is the identification of a set of criteria by which theories may be judged. Building and evaluating theories entail much the same kind of issue and procedure. A good theory is a growing theory; it has an ever extending range of application. Theories rest on data and data are generated by research. Thus a theory must be a rich source of hypotheses. These hypotheses must not be vague or indicate ambiguous outcomes; they must be empirically testable, i.e. potentially falsifiable. A good theory is usable, therefore it must be as parsimonious in terminology as is consistent with the power to explain. Testability entails that a good theory be internally consistent. For example, the definition of each term or relationship must not be a contradiction of the definition of any other term or relationship. These criteria, breadth of application, testability, parsimony, internal consistency and richness as a source of hypotheses, are each complex in themselves and related to each other. Below we expand on some of them.

The matter of judging the quality and progress of scientific theory is complex. Our discussion is necessarily brief and points only to the kinds of ideas which have guided our thinking on Piaget's theory. For more extensive discussions see Keat and Urry, 1975; Koch, 1959, 1974; Kuhn, 1970; and Lakatos and Musgrave, 1970.

Breadth of application

A theory may apply to a very limited set of data or it may be more general. Skinner's account of operant conditioning applied in the first instance to the behaviour of pigeons in specially constructed boxes but has since been used to give accounts of wide ranges of animals and human behaviour including the acquisition of language. This growth in the breadth of application of a theory is a manifestation of the generality of the concepts identified as fundamental. The concept of reinforcement, for example, has been shown by Skinner and his colleagues to be of quite general application. The generality of concepts cannot be judged in advance of their use. As a consequence, the more a theoretical proposition is applied and the more it seems to be sustained as useful, the more we assign it general significance.

There are no yardsticks for judging 'breadth of application'.

Testability

We have noted that we demand of a scientific theory that it can be used to generate predictions. Our degree of confidence in the validity of the theory is proportional to the degree to which these predictions are testable, i.e. informative. There is no point in generating predictions which are untestable. It is less than ideal to have predictions which are not potentially falsifiable. If a theory can be used to predict all possible outcomes of a situation then we are no better for having the theory than not. Such predictions carry no information value. A theory should be able to predict the presence of some outcomes and the absence of others. In this view a useful hypothesis is one which is, in principle, falsifiable.

The notion that science makes progress via theoretically based conjectures and empirically based refutations is not without problems and not without its critics. Suppose a hypothesis generated from the theory proves to be false. Do we reject the whole theory? Do we question those concepts used to generate the hypothesis? Do we treat it as measurement error? In testing any hypothesis there are probably many other hypotheses implicit in our measuring instruments or data analysis procedures. Could it be that one of these has been falsified? Clearly it is very difficult to know what to make of particular acts of falsification. This is not to say that falsification is an irrelevant criterion, rather that it is a very difficult notion with which to work.

There is the view however (Feyerabend, 1970) that progress via a process of conjecture and refutation is unnecessarily slow. In this view the essence of progress is industry. Sheer quantity of empirical work generates data which can be scrutinised for generality.

Parsimony

If we have a set of data or phenomena which we seek to describe and comprehend it seems self evident that the more rendered down the description is the more easily it can be accommodated intellectually. Of course this rendering down must not result in a loss of complexity or accuracy. By representing all forms of matter in terms of atoms the physicist has a very parsimonious way of describing a wide range of properties of matter and related phenomena such as magnetism and electricity. Additionally, this representation can readily be manipulated symbolically to explore relationships not amenable to inquiry if the concrete form of representation were the limit of our description.

Parsimony is related to breadth of application. The greater the range of phenomena that can be accommodated by a limited number of concepts the more powerful and efficient is our mode of representation. There is no absolute scale of parsimony. A theory can only be judged parsimonious in respect of other theories claiming to account for the same data. Equally, whilst efforts are made to remove redundant concepts in a theory and sharpen the definitions of others, there is no 'ideal' number of concepts to be striven for. Any appeal for parsimony must recognise the considerable complexity of the problems social science theories deal with. Simple theories are to be preferred to complex theories only when they are equally valid and general.

Fruitfulness

We have noted earlier that a good theory is a rich source of empirical work. This is so, but the proviso to be emphasised is that the work must be productive—it must have implications for the development of general theory. Industry is often confused with productivity. The advent of information processing theories in cognitive psychology has led to a massive surge in research but critics have recently noted that the majority of this work is not making a contribution to theoretical progress (Allport, 1975; Newell, 1974). The work is said to have become 'phenomena driven' rather than 'theory driven'. It seems that the theory is not amenable to direct, empirical investigation and as a consequence the data gathered have little clear implication for the development of theory.

Assessing Piaget's theory

In the above sections we have commented on the kinds of
question one must ask of a scientific theory. None of the
questions demands an absolute answer. Theories are judged in
some respects with reference to competing theories. In other
respects they are judged against our sense of scientific progress. In subsequent chapters we shall look at Piaget's theory
in detail with such issues in mind. In the second half of this
chapter we endeavour to locate Piaget's theory in the context
of other views of intellectual development. In that section we
focus on the issue we first nominated, that is the problem of
making choices about the kinds of question to ask and the
kinds of data to select.

Contrasting approaches to cognitive development

Bryant (1971) identified three approaches to cognitive development. There are those which focus on perception, those
which emphasise the development of language and those
which study logical development *per se.*

The work of Bower, 1974; Fantz, 1964; and Gibson *et al.*,
1962 exemplifies an approach via the study of perception. In
this view it is suggested that the infant is born with certain
abilities to distinguish shape, distance and colour. Development consists of gradual changes from relatively simple codes
for the identification of incoming data, to more sophisticated
ones as a result of experience. The task of the developmental
psychologist is then to determine exactly how the new dis-
tinctive features of stimuli come to be apprehended and
learned.

The effects of language acquisition have been emphasised
and studied by workers of quite different orientations (e.g.
Vygotsky, 1962; Kendler and Kendler, 1962). In different
ways both attempt to explain how language provides a symbol
system which enables the child to develop from direct and
immediate responses to specific stimuli towards a mediated
form of behaviour which is more flexible and adaptive.

Piaget's studies examine the transition from immediate

action to more reflective, logical processes. We shall describe his account in detail in Chapter 2. For the moment we note that each authority has selected a focal problem in the analysis of cognitive development which indicates a view of what is significant in this process. Furthermore, it will be shown that each has a theoretical position which implies or expresses a stance on the role of inherited characteristics, on the nature and use of experience and on the distinction between development as a qualitative or quantitative change.

Cognitive development and perception

Perception is concerned with the processing of data acquired through the senses. By far the greatest volume of research in this field has concentrated upon the visual sense, and this will be used in this section.

It has been demonstrated that very young infants possess some significant perceptual processes. Fantz (1964) has shown that at the age of five days they are able to distinguish certain common configurations of patterns, such as a human face, from stimuli containing the same pattern elements but in a scrambled form. The author was not arguing that there was an innate tendency to recognise the face, but that patterns with close similarities to social objects had properties identifiable to a newborn child.

Bower (1974), using infants of only a few weeks old, also demonstrated several perceptual competencies. Amongst them was the ability of the infant to discriminate between a small object moving close to the face and a larger object moving toward the face but from a safe distance (see Fig. 1.1). Even though both objects produced the same size image on the retina the infant only made a defensive reaction to the small, close object.

It is open to conjecture whether such perceptual abilities are present at birth, or whether they are learned very quickly indeed. There is no doubt, however, that the infant seems to have a considerable repertoire of perceptual skills. The manner in which these perceptual skills become modified during childhood has been the main interest of E. J. and J. J. Gibson. They argued that the young child tended to discriminate

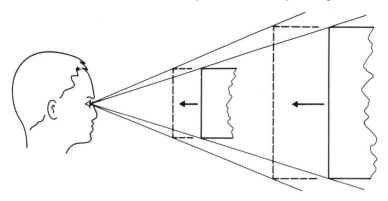

Figure 1.1   *Same size retinal images projected by objects at different distances (adapted from Bower, 1974)*

along a few dimensions which have particular relevance for him. Over a period of time other dimensions become relevant, and are incorporated into his perceptual processing. Typical of their experiments was that using the matching task shown in Fig. 1.2. Children of four and five years tended to match according to shape, irrespective of orientation. By the age of seven to eight years this additional feature had been added (Gibson *et al.*, 1962).

Spatial orientation is thus seen as an important development in the child's perceptual processing. Initially it has little relevance, they argue, because the fundamental acquisition of the notion of object permanence does not depend on orientation. That is, the child learns that Mummy remains the same Mummy whether she is far off or close at hand, and whether standing, sitting or lying down. Only when the child is faced

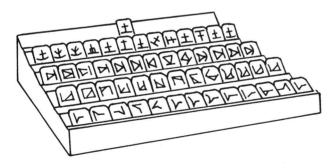

Figure 1.2   *A perceptual matching task (adapted from Bryant, 1971)*

with a new demand, that of decoding written symbols, does orientation become a salient feature, for only then does it actually alter the meaning of the perceived object.

This theoretical emphasis upon the perceptions of the child takes its evidence from his behaviour in specific tasks. However, it seems unlikely that the child of four years really fails in all situations to perceive orientation as relevant. He does not often try to feed the wrong end of a teddy bear, nor does he attempt to balance bricks or boxes without orienting them first. Bryant (1971) suggested that the complex array led to a selection of what could be remembered, not what was perceived, in the Gibsons' experiment. Analysis of his own experiments suggested that the failures were indeed in the ability of children adequately to represent orientation in memory, and were not indicative of the salience of certain features.

This does not invalidate the 'perceptual' approach by any means, though it does suggest that the emphasis should be placed upon researching the reason why some stimulus dimensions are more readily coded than others, and the manner in which new codes are developed. Thus the theoretical approach in which perception was given pre-eminence would seem to have been superseded by one studying the cognitive processes which give rise to the behaviour in perceptual tasks.

As a theoretical approach the perceptual studies fulfilled many of the criteria specified earlier. The basic thesis that the child's reactions to the environment would best be analysed through study of his perceptual processes is both plausible and logical. The predictions that his behaviour in perceptual experiments would provide indices of developmental trends, and that the introduction of new trends would be concomitant with new demands made by the environment, could be operationalised and tested. The weakness of the approach lay not so much in the invalidity of the claims as in the realisation that behaviour on perceptual tasks, and the very act of perceiving itself, is better construed as a cognitive process, of which sensory input and discriminatory behaviour are only a small part. The crucial aspects of processing appear to lie in processes which transform sensory input and give it meaning, and which then generate behaviour.

Focus on language: the behaviourists

Working within the behaviourist paradigm Howard and Tracy Kendler (1975) sought to explain cognitive development by studying the impact of language acquisition on cognition. They observed the different patterns of responses given to discrimination tests by children who possessed language and by those who did not.

Their studies derived from the work of Margaret Kuenne (1946). She presented a visual discrimination task to children between the ages of four and eight years. The stimuli consisted of a series of white squares of graded surface area. The children were first trained to respond consistently to one of an adjacent pair. Half of each age cohort were then presented with another pair consisting of one of the original pair and its adjacent square. The other half were given a new pair of stimuli from five steps along the sequence. These two procedures were referred to as 'near transposition' and 'far transposition' (see Fig. 1.3).

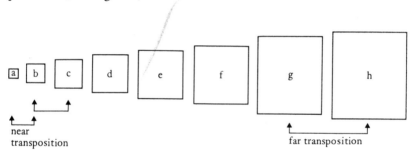

Figure 1.3   *Visual discrimination array (not to scale)*

A child who has been taught to select square *b* rather than *c* may have responded to the actual size of *b*, and may try to recognise that size again in another pair. This would be termed an *absolute* judgment. Alternatively he may respond to the relationship between *b* and *c*, and as *b* is smaller than *c* he would then look for a similar relationship in a new pair, this would be a *relative* judgment.

From Figure 1.3 it can be seen that children presented with a 'near transposition' task would again select *b* if they were making an absolute judgment, but would select *a* if making a relative judgment. In the far task only a relative judgment would be possible.

Kuenne found that the youngest of her children produced relative judgments on the 'near' task, but chose randomly on the 'far' task. She interpreted this as evidence that they were not making truly relational judgments. With older children there was increasing use of relative judgments on both tasks. These findings were interpreted in the light of a verbal mediation theory, in which the ability to use verbal cues such as 'choose the larger' enables the child to transcend the immediate impact of the stimulus.

Kendler and Kendler (1961) extended this procedure, training children of between five and six years to select the larger of two rectangles, irrespective of colour (see Fig. 1.4). They were then randomly divided into two groups, Group 1 having to select the smaller rectangle (a 'reversal shift'), and Group 2 having to select black (a 'non-reversal shift').

The Kendlers argued that if the concept had been acquired by a straightforward stimulus-response process, Group 2 should learn the new task more quickly, for some of the initial training had quite fortuitously involved rewarding the selection of black rectangles. Group 1 would be at a disadvantage as the selection of smaller rectangles had never been rewarded. On the other hand, if some internal mediation had taken place and the children were representing the idea of 'larger' to themselves, it might be easier for Group 1 to reverse the concept than for Group 2 to generate a new one.

In the sample as a whole neither proved more successful, but when the children's speed of learning the initial task was analysed it was discovered that fast learners succeeded in Group 1 and slow learners in Group 2. The authors explained this in the same way that Kuenne had done, by assuming that fast learners had superior verbal ability and were able to represent a mediating verbal concept to themselves. The slower children had not yet acquired that ability and were obliged to operate a more primitive and mechanistic stimulus-response process.

The focus upon acquisition of language in these studies is characteristic of verbal mediation theories. The shift from absolute codes, which are acquired by simple stimulus-response mechanisms, to relative codes, in which a language element intervenes, is seen as indicative of a shift from specific learning to conceptual learning. That is, the acquisition

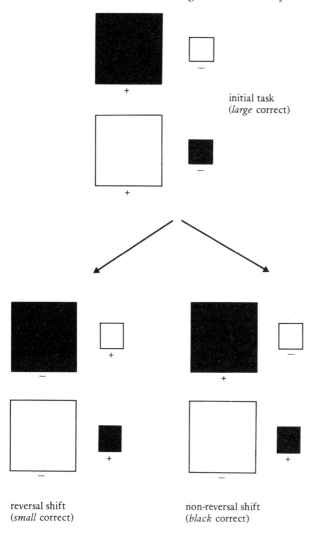

initial task
(*large* correct)

reversal shift   non-reversal shift
(*small* correct)   (*black* correct)

Figure 1.4   *Kendler's transposition experiment (adapted from Kendler and Kendler, 1962)*

of language allows more flexible behaviour presenting internal, mediating responses between stimulus and overt action.

There are a number of cogent criticisms relating to experimental procedures and alternate explanations of findings (see Bryant, 1971 and 1974); but perhaps the most important within the present context is that concerning the pre-eminent position afforded to language in these studies. The shift to relative codes is said to be *effected* by the acquisition of language. That is, when the child is able to say to himself 'choose the larger' he can transcend the arbitrary response to the individual stimulus and can operate at a conceptual level. Yet it is very difficult to imagine how the child can use the word 'larger' in any meaningful way *unless he is already able* to make judgments of 'larger' and 'smaller'. And if he can make judgments of that sort at a non-linguistic level he does not need a mediating verbal response to assist him.

However, it may be that language affords some benefits, in that it enables the child to store the discrimination in a readily accessible form for subsequent use (Kendler and Kendler, 1975). Here language is no longer necessarily implicated in the fundamental cognitive processes of discriminating dimensions, but takes on an important ancillary role in the utilisation of the acquired discriminatory acts.

Given that conditioning is an automatic process dependent upon external exigencies, and that mediating responses are similar in nature, it might be argued that no transition mechanism is required. That is, the emergence of mediating links (*s-r*) embedded in overt behavioural links (*S-R*) will be purely a matter of reinforcement. Yet the hypothesis that mediating responses interpose in efficiently functioning behaviours after a certain period of time does require an explanation. What causes *s-r* to emerge?

If language facilitates the storage and use of information there is a problem of how and when it is used. Osgood (1957) showed that verbally competent children sometimes responded in unsophisticated ways. In which case it is pertinent to ask why, if mediating responses exist, they are not always used.

The Kendlers admitted that 'the future development of the theory requires both a mechanism for the transition between levels and a more detailed theory of the nature of the encoding processes that characterise the mediational level' (1975, p. 221).

Although the Kendlers are customarily referred to as verbal mediation theorists, this is not the whole truth. They suggested that there may be several forms of internal mediation, one of which was language. However, this makes the situation even more complicated, for presumably other codes may give rise to relative judgments in the absence of a linguistic code. We are led to conclude that, whilst verbal behaviour is undoubtedly implicated in the cognitive development of the child, it is difficult to ascribe it a role on the basis of the kinds of study executed by the Kendlers.

Focus on language: A. R. Luria

A rather different approach to the place of language in cognitive development is presented by Luria (1961) and others of the Soviet Interactionist School. The initial assumption of the importance of language, and its function as an intervening, superordinate system has much in common with that proposed by the Kendlers (above).

Luria's work is associated with that form of Soviet psychology known as sociohistorical development (Sahakian, 1975). It proposes that language is a tool which the child learns to use in order to regulate behaviour: 'the most significant moment in the course of intellectual development, which gives birth to the purely human forms of practical and abstract intelligence, occurs when speech and practical activity, two previously completely independent lines of development, converge' (Vygotsky: in Cole *et al.*, 1978).

Luria's work was essentially a development of this same line, suggesting that the human brain develops two interdependent mechanisms. One of these is relatively primitive, being made up of simple reflex actions which, by conditioning, can become extended and elaborated. The other is much more elaborate, containing a complex of concepts derived from experience. To this extent it closely resembles the behaviourist approach. Like the Kendlers, Luria asserted that the higher system is not solely linguistic in nature.

The crucial difference appears to lie in the manner in which this higher system is conceptualised. To the behaviourists it constitutes an alternate pattern of stimuli and responses which may be interposed between the basic *S-R* connections. In origin it is identical, being the product of reinforcing agencies. Luria, however, places no such limitation upon the higher system.

Stimulation of sensory receptors may lead to motor output, but the higher system can interpose in the form of a functional barrier. In the adult all incoming signals would normally pass through this barrier before output was possible. The relationship between the two systems is envisaged as a dynamic one in which activation of the two leads to constant adaptation and modification. The manner in which this functional barrier developed, particularly in its linguistic form, was the task to which Luria and his colleagues addressed themselves.

Luria (1959) pointed out that the young child's responses to verbal commands and requests were often unpredictable. In one experiment a child was placed before two toys, a brightly coloured cat placed near to him and a toy fish further away. A verbal request to retrieve the fish caused orientation and stretching toward the fish, but the action would be interrupted by the powerful visual influence of the cat. As a consequence of the strong bond between visual stimulus and action the cat would be retrieved instead of the fish. In this way Luria sought to illustrate that at an early age the directive function of language was not maintained in the presence of more powerful sensory stimulation of the lower system.

By about the age of eighteen months the external verbal command would be sufficiently powerful to orient the child and cause him to complete the desired activity. Full verbal regulation would still not have been achieved however, for once a command had indicated action another command could not inhibit it. It would be more likely to intensify the action.

A typical illustration of this phenomenon involved an apparatus consisting of flashing red and blue lights and a rubber ball which was connected to a recording device. The verbal instruction 'when the red light flashes press the bulb' was given. This was a complex instruction involving a conditional plan for future action. It was reported that between the ages of nineteen months and two years children did not recognise the conditional nature of the instruction. Mention of the light caused them to look expectantly towards it, and 'press the bulb' elicited immediate motor action. In short, the verbal stimuli had only immediate triggering effects.

By the fourth year this pattern was shown to have changed, so that the conditional instruction initiated correct behaviour. Once again, action begun tended to be continued irrespective of subsequent changes to the lights, although this could be counteracted by interpolating a reminder in the form of further verbal interjection or by using simple rules such as 'always leave go of the bulb after the light has flashed'.

From the age of four years the functioning of the higher system would become more complete, so that a truly regulatory system to external commands would develop. From this would emerge an internal self-regulatory system as internalised speech forms provided the means.

Luria's explanation of this sequence hinged upon the relative effects of the lower and higher systems interacting. For the very young child the excitation of the lower system, in terms of perceptual impact or motor activity, was strong. The excitation of the higher 'verbal' system was, however, strictly limited because of the small number of neural connections which had been made. For this reason it was said to have 'low mobility'.

This inclusion of neural correlates and explanations marked a clear divergence from the behaviourists. The fact that the child may understand the 'light-press' instruction but still be unable to operationalise it was explained in the following way. The excitation produced by the visual signal was so strong, and so diffuse, that it carried over to that portion of the cortex dealing with perception of the blue light, causing a response to be evoked to that too. The inhibitory effect of the verbal instruction was too weak to counteract it. The efficiency of various forms of intervention resided in their introducing additional excitation after the response had been made. This conflicted with the existing excitation from the original stimulus and blocked its effect.

In its earliest form this linguistic effect was seen merely as a substitute for the excitation of the lower system, rather than a regulatory mechanism with a separate identity. That is, the words produced more powerful stimulation. This was used to explain why, when children were asked to say 'press' or 'don't press' as they manipulated the rubber ball, both utterances were found to elicit bulb-pressing. That is, the words functioned as stimuli for 'impulsive' behaviour, their semantic content was ignored (Luria, 1961).

When the linguistic system had forged sufficient neural connections, that is, had become mobile, its function changed. It would then mediate most of the lower system's activity prior to response. The semantic content of the words was now seen as assuming importance. As soon as this began to happen 'external speech became superfluous. The directive role is taken over by those inner connections which lie behind the word . . .' (Luria, 1959, p. 80).

Luria's theory is logically consistent. Its weakness lies primarily in its reliance upon the hypothetical relationships of psychological behaviour and neural activity. In this respect Luria seems guilty of premature physiologising, since the neural mechanisms underlying simple behaviours are quite unclear at the present time. Furthermore, in postulating a separate 'higher' system and describing its effects in terms of excitation and inhibition, Luria's theory is inconsistent with modern physiological studies indicating complex and diffuse cerebral activity (Milner, 1970).

A further weakness lies in the absence of an adequate explanation of how the impulse-semantic transition of word effect takes place. Unlike Kendler's model, which assumes that both systems are built up by means of an identical process—establishing S-R bonds—Luria's treatment of the higher system made no such assumptions. His explanations were couched in very general, non-specific terms which make systematic investigation difficult.

Various attempts to evaluate the theory have been made (see Bloor, 1977). Miller, Shelton and Flavell (1970) tested the hypothesis that 3-year-old children should best perform motor tasks in silence, and that subsequently overt verbalisation should have an impulsive effect and later a regulatory effect. They failed to confirm this, as did Jarvis (1963) and Wilder (1968), and concluded that motor and verbal tasks appeared to operate independently.

Piaget's theory

Piaget became interested in child psychology in order to explore the nature of knowledge. He refers to his area of study as 'genetic epistemology'. 'Epistemology' is the study of knowledge and the adjective 'genetic' denotes his interest in its origins and the ways in which it develops.

Piaget assumes that if he knows how knowledge is constructed then he should know something about what knowledge is, because the construction of knowledge reflects the nature of knowledge, just as the construction of a chair reflects what a chair is (Furth, 1977, p. 66).

Piaget's theory may be described in terms of an analogy between the physical laws which govern living organisms and the laws which govern intellectual activity. Biological survival may be construed as comprising two complementary activities, adaptation and organisation. These are the functionally invariant processes of biological and intellectual life.

Adaptation is subdivided into assimilation and accommodation. Assimilation refers to the 'taking in' of material from the environment (e.g. the ingestion of food). Accommodation refers to modifications made by the organism in order to use the assimilated materials. At the psychological level, the analogy supposes information from the environment is assimilated by the mind and changes occur within the existing mental structures in order to accommodate the new information.

The process of organisation requires changes in the underlying mental structures which mediate the organism's interchanges with the environment. The changes involve increasing degrees of sophistication as development proceeds and they permit the individual to attain ever more mobile and general states of equilibrium. Efficient cognitive development depends upon an appropriate match of experience and existing cognitive structures. This optimal match permits equilibration to take place. The complementary processes of assimilation and accommodation lead to a form of mental balance called an equilibrium state. Additional, dissonant information, when assimilated, requires further accommodation leading to further processes of equilibration and the construction of a 'higher' equilibrium state.

Piaget's theory is also a *structuralist* theory. The systematic changes which occur as a result of equilibration give rise to a series of *stages*, the structures of which may be observed in behaviours as disparate as language, moral reasoning, problem solving, perception, and play. These stages have a necessary and invariant sequence, stemming originally from physical action but moving by a complex process of reconstruction to increasingly sophisticated mental structures.

Throughout childhood, the course of cognitive development may be summarised as increasing emancipation from perception. As the child interacts with his environment he develops increasingly sophisticated mental capacities which enable him to go beyond mere response to the observable features of a problem. The logical rules which the child formulates to permit this development are the central focus of Piaget's work. One example from a vast body of published work will suffice to illustrate his procedures.

The mental processes of the young child are characterised by *egocentricity*. In the 'three mountain problem' (Piaget and Inhelder, 1956) a child is shown a model of three mountains with various distinguishing features. When a doll is placed at some other angle to the model the child is unable to select a photograph which represents the doll's view. Instead he tends to select his own view. From the age of about eight years this no longer happens. Piaget contends that by that age the child has developed mental representations which can be operated upon with logical rules. Immediate perception is no longer dominant. Many other responses to problems will also be changing at the same time. The child will be moving from a stage with one type of characteristic structure to another of more complex structure.

As a theory this view has much to commend it. It has a high level of internal consistency, wide field of application, and in some respects, is capable of empirical exploration in that the presence or absence of certain cognitive structures is predicted by it.

Intellectual development and the role of experience

The multifarious changes which constitute child development are of great interest, and there is much to be gained by describing them. As we have seen, these descriptions do not of themselves afford a theory of development. To meet that requirement we need, in addition to the formal requirements of any theory, a description of how changes come about. There is little controversy over the observed differences which occur in perceptual, verbal or problem solving behaviour. Nor is there doubt that in most children these processes run concurrently. What is in contention is which offers the best source of information on the developmental process, and how much emphasis should be given to the role of experience.

The Gibsons emphasised the manner in which experience refined and modified perceptual processes which were inherited. The principal weakness of their work lay in taking for granted the salience of particular perceptual cues. As we have seen, examination of this notion takes us out of the field of perception into more central cognitive processing.

The crucial difference between the Gibsons and Piaget is that Piaget uses perception and action only as a starting point from which cognitive processes develop, which ultimately transcend perception.

To the Kendlers experience constitutes the total formative influence on development. Behavioural repertoires are entirely dependent upon contingent reinforcement. Only one process is invoked to explain the overt behavioural development of the pre-linguistic child and the mediated behaviour of the child with language. It was shown that there were grave problems in assigning such importance to language, and the Kendlers have been obliged to relegate it from a central role in the acquisition of concepts to that of a facilitator of performance. This too is more in line with Piaget's view that language developments always succeed equivalent changes in cognitive structures.

Luria's position, although superficially similar to that of the Kendlers, is nearer to that of the Gibsons with regard to the influence of experience. Initial responses are developed to perceptually salient features of the environment. Experience serves to modify the neural activity, giving rise to more flexible behaviour patterns.

Piaget's theory emphasises the way in which the learner is active in constructing developmental change by deriving information from the environment and using it to modify and elaborate existing mental processes. For this process to operate efficiently there must be a close relationship between the existing mental structures and the structure of the new experiences. That is, experience *per se* is not necessarily beneficial.

Chapter 2

Piaget's theory of cognitive development

In this chapter we provide a résumé of Piaget's theory as a framework for subsequent commentary. Illustrative material abounds in Piaget's own writings and in the work of his best-known expositors (e.g. Flavell, 1963). In the interests of brevity it will be omitted from these pages.

An ideal theory of cognitive development must offer descriptions of mental contents at various points in the development sequence. These descriptions will represent all the rules and knowledge necessary to fulfil the performance characteristics of the organism. The descriptions will be of the underlying competence of the organism (Chomsky, 1972; Flavell and Wohlwill, 1969). To explain particular behavioural acts or performances an ideal theory must also offer a set of rules describing how underlying competence is made manifest and the kinds of organismic and task variables which would elicit or impede performance. Finally, the theory must offer an account of how developmental change comes about. In this chapter we look in detail at Piaget's theory with the above requirements in mind. We present Piaget's view without critical comment. It is our intention to focus key issues here and explore them more fully in subsequent chapters.

Piaget sees psychological development as analogous to biological epigenesis (Piaget, 1970a, 1971a). A few remarks on this process may help an understanding of Piaget's theory. There appear to be four features essential to epigenesis (Kitchener, 1978). First, the process involves a causal sequence of events. In a sequence of steps $S_1, S_2 \ldots S_n, S_1$ causes S_2, S_2 causes S_3 and so on. Second the sequence involves increasing differentiation, complexity and organisation. There is a transformation from homogeneous to heterogeneous

22

states and from general to specific functions. Also, 'the theory of epigenesis, whatever else it may imply, asserts that development is *not* simply a question of increase of scale . . . but a process in which a genuine increase in "complexity" is progressively achieved' (Woodger, quoted in Kitchener, 1978, p. 147).

Third, the notion of *emergence* is an underlying principle of epigenesis. With progress towards complexity something new emerges at each step. Qualitatively different structures appear. The fourth notion implicit in epigenesis is that it involves a stepwise growth through a series of stages. Each stage is marked by the qualitatively different emergent structures noted above. Fundamental questions raised by this (epigenetic) view of development include,

(a) What properties characterise each stage?
(b) What is the goal of the entire process?
(c) What processes are involved in transforming one stage into another?

These questions are central to discovering the general laws of development.

Other questions may be asked about individuality or individual differences. These questions raise the issue of the role of environmental factors in epigenesis. With respect to biological theory it is not at all clear what role environmental factors play in the course of development. We will return to the role of environmental factors later in this chapter.

The stages of development in Piaget's theory

What properties characterise each stage? We have identified this as a question fundamental to an understanding of development. The greater part of Piaget's writings describe sequential development in modes of thinking which may be construed in distinct stages, within each of which there is a common cognitive structure. The nature of these structures is described either in terms of the principle by which they are formed or by means of the algebra of symbolic logic. There are four major stages, namely the sensori-motor, the preconceptual, the concrete operational and the formal operational stage.

The sensori-motor stage

This stage is described largely in terms of the processes which produce its structures.

Sub-Stage 1 (0–1 month)

The infant reacts by means of a series of innate reflexes, which constitute the basic materials for all subsequent development. Accommodation appears almost immediately in that the sucking reflex becomes modified so that it is stimulated more easily and the nipple more readily located. It should be noted that this is actually a modification to the preparatory activity rather than the sucking, but this is in keeping with Piaget's interpretation of a schema constituting the initiating stimuli of events, the organism's reaction to them, and the ensuing behaviour.

The self-motivating aspect of a schema is also demonstrated by the infant's generalisation to sucking other objects.

Sub-Stage 2 (1–4 months)

A small though significant change in accommodation occurs when the infant systematically sucks the thumb. This is no longer an accidental generalisation as in Stage 1, but a new, learned behavioural pattern. The term *circular reaction* is used to denote a sequence which is initiated by a chance response, but which, by a process of assimilation which is inherent in the infant, tends to be repeated. At this stage these reactions are focused upon the infant's body, not on the surrounding environment; these are *primary circular reactions*.

Similar developments occur in other behaviours, particularly seeing, grasping and vocalisation. There is also a significant emergence of integrated patterns of responses, as in the combination of seeing and grasping. However, the objects grasped at seem to be represented only in the act itself. There appears to be no awareness of objective reality which would admit of the object's existence outside the act. This illustrates also the essential *egocentricity* of the whole period.

Sub-Stage 3 (4–8 months)

In this stage *secondary circular reactions* emerge. They differ from the primary form since they modify motor habits, not reflexes, and because they now encompass elements of the infant's environment, as well as his own body. The first indication of object permanence also appears at this stage. Visual search will be instigated for objects which have been removed from his field of vision.

Interest and activity which involves events outside the child give rise to what Flavell calls 'the first sensori-motor analogues of classes and relations' (p. 104). Hence the rattle is an example of things which involve shaking and hearing noise.

Piaget also discusses other forms of assimilation in this stage. In response to a familiar object the infant may 'recognise' it by performing a perfunctory version of his usual motor behaviour, yet with apparently no intentions of actually reacting with it. That is, his activity is a form of motor recognition. This is to be distinguished from a total reaction which the infant might exert in an attempt to maintain some distant aspect of the environment, even when to the observer it is clear that there is no causal relationship between the activity and the event.

A half-way stage to intentionality is apparent at this time. Initial behaviours tend to be fortuitous, but having produced an interesting effect, that becomes a goal for secondary circular reactions. This can be distinguished from intentionality proper, in which the goal is known before actions commence.

Sub-Stage 4 (8–12 months)

Secondary circular reactions become co-ordinated to form new, more complex *secondary schemas*. Furthermore, there is clear indication of genuine intention in which schemas are implemented with a view to achieving a goal. This can be seen when the infant commences an act, only to find it blocked by some obstruction which must be removed before the goal may be attained.

Infants in this stage show anticipatory behaviour. Their responses indicate that when a door opens someone will be there, and when certain receptacles appear that food will be presented. This is not to imply any sophisticated imagery, the index or signal is a part of the forthcoming event and as such is still closely bound to the infant's own sensori-motor behaviour, but it is a sign none the less (Piaget, 1950).

The notion of object permanence is also extended by the

development of superior manipulative skills. Being able to hold, turn and push objects around contributes to the discovery that objects are not changed, though their orientation and appearance may be.

Sub-Stage 5 (12–18 months)

In this period the circular reactions move into a new phase. *Tertiary circular reactions* are not easily distinguished from the secondary form. The child will still find unexpected consequences of his actions, and will still initiate circular repetitions in order to accommodate the new discovery. The difference is said to be in the degree of variation which accompanies the actions. Secondary reactions have an almost magical quality, in that the goal is achieved by initiation of a stereotyped behaviour pattern. In tertiary reactions there appears to be exploration of the events which achieve the goal. That is, the child will experiment with the relationship of action to goal.

This search for novel events represents the clearest and most obvious distinction between accommodation and assimilation. All previous stages have been primarily assimilating, although this is not entirely so, and it may be better to use the word 'adaptatory'. There must now be provision for modifying existing schemas with each act of investigation or experiment. Furthermore there will be an increased emphasis on the qualities of the object or event, separate from those of the perceiver. In other words, egocentrism is further diminished and the object concept strengthened.

The concept of object permanence also develops. A hidden object will be sought in the place where it was seen to be hidden whereas previously it was always sought in its usual place. This new ability will still not permit the child to search for an object which he has not seen hidden however.

Sub-Stage 6 (18–24 months)

The most sophisticated activity, by definition, emerges in the final part of the stage. The sequences of exploratory action which characterised sub-stage 5 now become covert. Instead of a series of external behaviours aimed at solving a problem, this can now be undergone internally, and prior to a selected action.

In order to achieve this dramatic effect the child must be

able to represent events to himself. It will be recalled that in sub-stage 4 an external event could act as a symbol which generated anticipatory behaviour. Now, some twelve months later, the child can represent some aspects of his environment as motor or mental images. 'Thought' is now interpretable in its more conventional form, as distinct from the earlier form of 'thought-as-action'.

Mental imagery now reaches a more sophisticated and complete form in the concept of object permanence. An object is now 'seen as an entity in its own right which exists and moves in a space common both to it and to the subject who observes it' (Flavell, p. 129). The child will now search for objects which he cannot see, and has not seen hidden, suggesting the existence of mental images of these objects.

The pre-operational stage

This stage covers approximately the years from two to seven. It is often described as containing two phases, the preconceptual or symbolic sub-stage (roughly two to four years) and the intuitive sub-stage (roughly four to seven years). Whilst it is clearly the case that dramatic changes occur between the age of two and seven years, there is felt to be a sufficiently pronounced *structure d'ensemble* to merit the designation of this span as a stage, and for that reason the overall changes will be described here without reference to the internal divisions.

Representations

Sub-stage 6 of the sensori-motor stage witnessed the emergence of rudimentary mental imagery. The pre-operational stage is characterised by extensive development of this phenomenon, such that intelligence is no longer manifest by overt acts, but increasingly by covert, symbolic manipulation of events.

It will be recalled that, at an earlier stage, the child was able to anticipate an event from the perception of a sign. That sign was an integral part of the event which it represented. For example, the presence of a dish indicated forthcoming food. Now a genuine *symbolic function* begins to emerge; that is, an ability to evoke an internal *signifier* which symbolises the *significate*. The crucial difference is said to lie in the origin and nature of the signifier. It is no longer a portion of the objective event, it is an internally generated representation, and as such it is no longer tied to events perceived, but can encompass past and future events, and has the mobility to incorporate many physically disparate features of the environment.

Mental symbols are thought to originate in the child's capacity to imitate. The young infant is capable of copying the acts of others, and during the second year of life this imitation may be deferred, i.e. it may be reproduced some time after the model has disappeared. This suggests that the child can represent the act in some internal form which is differentiated from the act itself.

Imitation demands changes to existing schemas in order to copy an external model. It is, therefore, a process of accommodation. Deferred imitations on the other hand, whilst undeniably requiring accommodation, require it in a somewhat different form. Now the signifier (as part of the schema) must evoke, as well as replicate, the model event. There is, therefore, wide scope for the generation of highly individual and personalised representations.

It will be apparent that equilibrium states attained during imitation in the sensori-motor period are relatively straightforward, demanding the equilibration of acts of assimilation and accommodation on contemporaneous events. Deferred imitation must employ processes across time; that is, assimilation of present events and/or evoked meanings, and accommodation to present events and/or past imitations and images.

The development of signifiers as personalised, internal *symbols* is a considerable advance upon the ability to identify a signal as a precursor of an event. Nevertheless it is suggested that these symbols do bear some physical relationship to the events they represent. The emergence of arbitrary *signs* with meanings agreed by consensus (such as words) occurs later, and only after a transition period in which words may be used as *semisigns*; that is, in personalised form and in conjunction with personal symbols.

Limitations of pre-conceptual thought

Although the pre-operational child does not have to act upon environmental events, but can represent them, these representations are thought to be quite close to the overt actions they have replaced. Herein lies one of the limitations of this stage. The child's cognition tends to be 'an isomorphic, step-by-step mental replica of concrete actions and events . . . the young child simply runs off reality sequences in his head just as he might do in overt action' (Flavell, 1963, p. 158). The child's representation of an event is likely to be of its immediate perceptual characteristics; those which would previously have stimulated his action.

An associated feature of the child's mental limitations is the inability to *decentre*, that is, to take account of different aspects of a phenomenon. The pre-operational child centres on a single, prominent feature and makes his judgments on that basis. In the well-known conservation of liquid volume experiment (Piaget, 1952), the height or the breadth of the liquid columns commands the child's attention, to the exclusion of compensatory variations in the other dimension.

Other descriptions of limitations overlap considerably with that in the previous paragraph. A true cognitive organisation is in relatively stable equilibrium, and is in accordance with the *principle of reversibility*. The instability of the pre-conceptual child's cognitive organisation is indicated by the ease with which transformations of displays lead him to disrupt brief states of equilibrium with contradictory conclusions. Furthermore, because internal representations mirror earlier action sequences, the child's understanding is limited to these sequences which have occurred. The symbolic reversal of a process (such as the return of liquid from a wide vessel to the original tall one, thereby affirming the invariance of the material) is beyond his competence.

Language development has already been mentioned with reference to the developing symbolic functions of this sub-stage. As a form of interpersonal communication however, it is still limited. The egocentricity of action noted in the sensori-motor stage still exists, and one of its manifestations is in communication (Piaget, 1926). The child is not thought to modify his speech to suit the needs of his listener, nor to conceive of the need to justify his reasoning. In fact, his thought processes do not seem available to him for analysis. He cannot retrace an argument or examine it for inconsistency.

The customary rules of logical reasoning require either that a general conclusion be reached from particular premises—a process of induction, or that a particular conclusion be derived from general premises—a process of deduction. Piaget refers to the reasoning of the preconceptual child as *transductive*, proceeding from particular to particular. Having centred upon prominent features of events, the child then draws some conclusion from them by a process of contiguity or similarity rather than logical correctness.

The items to which this reasoning is applied are described as *preconcepts*. As previously described the representations are closely related to actions and perceptual features, unlike the more abstract and schematic forms of later years. They tend to be idiosyncratic, neither consistently recognising the identity of an object in different contexts, nor consistently recognising that members of a group or class will have individual identities. In other words the rules governing individual uniqueness and class membership are sporadically and inconsistently applied; the distinctions of 'all', 'one' and 'some' are unclear.

Developmental changes

The preconceptual or symbolic sub-stage from two to four years is so called because of the marked growth in the symbolic function. This leads to behaviour which is increasingly characteristic of this sub-stage as described above. In the last three years thinking becomes more anticipatory of the operational form which will succeed it. The first appearances of decentring and reversibility occur, and thought processes become more readily directed. It is these partially directed but somewhat haphazard thought processes which the term 'Intuitive' is intended to convey.

The concrete operational period

Out of the intuitive thinking of the previous sub-stage there develops a much more complete and integrated mode for the use of representations. Assimilation and accommodation achieve a much greater degree of equilibrium. A more enduring and flexible set of mental mechanisms exists which is less easily thrown into confusion by the appearance of outside events.

These highly organised mental processes are called *operations*, and they are thought not to emerge before the seventh year. A great deal of Piaget's writings, particularly his earlier works, consist of highly detailed descriptions of the emergence of the logical operations of adding, multiplying, correspondence, etc., and the infralogical operations which are involved in manipulation of quantity, time, space, etc. (see Piaget, 1957a).

These processes do not merely accumulate. It is suggested that their use only makes sense as part of an integrated, overall structure, a *structure d'ensemble*. That is, to implement the notion of a class of objects implies a wider organisation of schemas involving class operations. Consequently the emergence of these operations is taken to imply that a total structure of inter-related operations exists. Many of these may not yet have been externalised, but they exist as *latent* or *potential* operations (Inhelder and Piaget, 1958). This *structure d'ensemble* is described in terms of a logico-mathematical model (Piaget, 1949).

The logico-mathematical model

As intellectual behaviour becomes increasingly diverse and complex, any efficient attempt at describing it is likely to focus on general rather than specific properties of mental acts. Such descriptions are likely to involve reference to terms such as 'rules', 'programmes', 'operations' and the like. These terms transcend particular overt behaviours. Such descriptions however must be envisaged as enduring 'mental possessions' of the thinker. The specification of such rules, plans or operations involves documenting the knowledge and its mode of representation necessary to the performance of a particular mental act. In this sense, describing general processes underlying intellectual behaviour is to describe *intellectual competence* (in Chomsky's sense). Just as linguistic competence does not represent the operations involved in processing sentences, the term intellectual competence does not provide

a description of the psychological processes involved in carrying out an act of cognition, but a description of the knowledge
and processes which must be pre-requisite to performing such
acts.

Faced with the problem of representing the organisation of
the knowledge and processes of mental life at each stage in
development and committed to viewing intellectual development as the epigenesis of logical structures, Piaget has chosen
to describe these contents in logical form. Below we lay out
in part his description of the concrete and formal operational
stages. The notation used seems a strange representation of
any individual act of reasoning. It must be emphasised therefore that what is evidently being offered by Piaget is a
description of the general, underlying competence necessary
to particular mental acts. Even if a particular person were in
possession of this competence all manner of task and organismic factors might impede the solution of a task requiring this
necessary competence.

In offering symbolic logic as a model of intellectual competence Piaget is attempting to reduce a bewildering array of
intellectual contents to its canonical form. He is offering a
model of the elements of cognition in structuralist terms.
This entails specifying the fundamental elements of acts of
cognition and defining the relationships which can occur
between the elements. Piaget considers that acts of cognition
have, at their base, a set of elements and processes isomorphic
with the elements and processes which describe certain logico-
mathematical domains. Our understanding of these domains
enables us to represent and comprehend the cognitive competence of the concrete operational and formal operational
stages. Below we set out a brief account of the domains Piaget
takes as isomorphic with cognition in these stages.

A mathematical *set* is a collection of *elements* (objects,
actions, ideas, etc.) which share some common property. It
may be infinitely large, such as the set of all human movements, or extremely small, such as the set of even numbers,
between 2 and 6. A special sort of set, in which any pair
of elements is related by a *rule of combination* is known as
a *group*. The rule of combination states that when an operation is performed upon the pair, the following rules must be
obeyed:

   1 *The rule of closure (or composition)* Any operation

combining two elements in the set must result in an element within the set.

2 *The rule of associativity* The combination of elements within the set must hold irrespective of the order in which they are treated.

3 *The identity rule* There must be one element only which, in combination with any other element leaves it unchanged.

4 *The inverse rule* For each element in the set there must be another which in combination with it, results in the identity element.

A *lattice* is a structure of similar type. It again consists of elements and involves a relation between any two or more elements. To comply with requirements of a lattice the relation between two or more elements must provide a *least upper bound* (l.u.b.); that is, a smallest element which includes all of them; and a *greatest lower bound* (g.l.b.), which is the largest element that is included in both.

Consider the following:

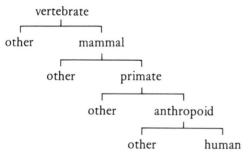

In the pair primate-mammal the l.u.b. is mammal (which incorporates primate), and the g.l.b. primate (which is the largest class in both). The same relationships obtain for any pair in the hierarchy, and it is therefore, a lattice.

Piaget combines most characteristics of these two to form a structure called a *grouping*, and this he uses to describe the cognitive structure of the first period of operations, which spans the years seven to eleven (Piaget, 1942). This work operates at two levels. At the empirical level Piaget appears to be suggesting that groupings offer the best framework in which to construe the variety of concrete operations which the child acquires. At the abstract level he is setting out a logical structure which accommodates the nature of class membership and relations between elements. An appropriate analogy might be to suggest that the child behaves as though he constructed routines made up of these logical structures.

There are eight major groupings of logical classes and relations. These are: I primary addition of classes, II secondary addition of classes, III bi-universal multiplication of classes, IV co-universal multiplication of classes, V addition of asymmetrical relations, VI addition of symmetrical relations, VII bi-universal multiplication of relations, VIII co-universal multiplication of relations. There is also a preliminary grouping of equalities, sometimes classed as the ninth grouping, but more properly a basic grouping which occurs within the other eight. An example of one grouping will serve to illustrate how it is thought to relate to the child's cognitive behaviour.

Grouping III: bi-universal multiplication of classes

If we consider the class of people P_p, we can divide them into subclasses; *men* (A), *women* (B), and *children* (C). Then $A + B + C = P_p$.

Alternatively we could divide them according to skin colour; *fair* (F), *medium* (G), and *dark* (H): such that $F + G + H = P_s$.

Within these two classes it is possible to multiply sub-classes together. Thus $B \times H$ gives us the class of dark skinned women (that is the intersect of B and H, or $B \supset H$).

In fact the whole of the two series of sub-classes can be multiplied, and the products of elements could be entered in a 3 X 3 matrix. This multiplicative relationship between all sub-classes is represented by the term *bi-universal*. However, the system is not limited to two classes, and can easily be extended to further dimensions.

		P_p		
		A	B	C
P_s	F	AF	BF	CF
	G	AG	BG	CG
	H	AH	BH	CH

As groupings must meet all the requirements of logical groups, these can be tested on this example.

The rule of closure or composition

None of the products in the table fall outside the classes P_p or P_s: they are all groups of people with skin colour.

The rule of associativity

$A \times F = F \times A$, the order is unimportant. *Men* $\times$ *fair-skin* is the same as *fair-skin* $\times$ *men.*

The identity rule

Every sub class is the identity element for itself. That is, $A \times A = A$, $F \times F = F$. This is sometimes referred to as the *tautology* property.

The inverse rule

The division of products is the inverse operation which results in the identity element (i.e. the process reverses the multiplication of sub-classes).
$A \times F = AF$, *men* $\times$ *fair-skin* = *fair-skinned men.*
$AF \div F = A$, *fair-skinned men* $\div$ *fair-skin* = *men.*

All other groupings operate in similar ways (see Flavell, 1963). Groupings I and II encompass the rules for the addition and subtraction of classes, Groupings III and IV for their multiplication and division. The remainder are concerned with the relationships which may be found between classes, or elements of classes, e.g. asymmetrical relations such as 'greater than', 'the son of', etc.; and symmetrical relations such as 'sister of' (between two or more females).

Piaget's view is that the child, between the ages of seven and eleven years, shows evidence of functioning indicative of a cognitive structure which may be represented by these groupings. In particular, the inverse rule in the form of reversibility is repeatedly emphasised as a criterion *par excellence* of cognitive operations. That these structures are manifest, at first, only in mental actions which involve the concrete, perceivable world accounts for the term concrete operations. As the period progresses there will be actions which utilise symbolic material and which consider potentialities rather than actualities, but these are the exception rather than the rule.

Examples of concrete operational behaviour, from which the groupings are readily discerned, include the following (Piaget and Inhelder, 1969):

Transitive inference

The ability to seriate objects according to some dimension (e.g. length) emerges in a primitive form in pre-operations, but becomes truly operative when the child understands that the implications of placing E after D in the series $A > B > C > D$ is that E is not only less than D, but also less than all others. Furthermore, it is reciprocally greater than F, G or H. When this operation is achieved, the child is able, without making a direct comparison, to infer that, if $A > B$ and $B > C$, then $A > C$. This operation is seen as an example of behaviour which can be represented by Grouping V.

Classification

Pre-operational children are well able to classify objects with which they are familiar. If asked to show 10 buttons, of which 6 are white and 4 red, they can do this. They can also go on to show the 4 red ones when requested. When asked 'are there more buttons or more red ones?' he is likely to give an erroneous response. In thinking of the sub-class 'red-ones' he fails to conserve the class 'buttons'. With the operational child this does not occur. By about eight years of age the child can handle even more complex classes in which more than one type of sub-class is present—a mixture of red and white circles and squares for instance. These operations are said to be represented by Grouping I for the first instance and Grouping III for the second.

Conservation of quantity, length, etc.

The conservation studies, which are the most widely used examples of concrete operational thought, display structures of Grouping VII. These involve the conservation of some property (length, volume, mass, etc.) between two objects when some transformation occurs to one of them. Thus, when water is transferred from a tall thin vessel to a short, wide one the relations 'shorter than' and 'wider than' must be seen to be multiplied together.

In addition there are a number of *infra-logical* structures which emerge at the same time as the logical ones that have been discussed. They are related to estimations of continuous quantities, and, by employing operations which involve the partitioning of the whole quantity in its estimation, they have structures which are similar to, but not identical with, the groupings listed above. The estimation of length is reported to entail the interpretation of the whole as a series of equal units, and the calculation of the number of times a unit would fit into the whole. The process has much in common with Groupings I and V.

Pinard and Laurendeau (1969) conclude that the *structure d'ensemble* of the concrete operational stage is to be found in the interdependence of the logical groupings. The utilisation of a structure based upon one grouping implies, logically, an ability to utilise all the other groupings with which it is isomorphic. The logic of this is to be found in the fact that all groupings are based upon the same combination of fundamental operations.

The formal operational stage

In the final period of intellectual development the cognitive processes become 'formalised' in the sense that they became detached from the concrete material in which they originated. Just as concrete operations represented a major advance in the treatment of external events by their integration into stable, mobile structures, formal operations are an advance because they are not restricted to dealing with data, but take the products of concrete operations as a starting point out of which evolves 'second-order' operations.

These 'second-order' operations are able to deal not only with the events of the real world, but also with possible events. 'Reality is thus conceived as a special subset within the totality of things which the data would admit as hypotheses; it is seen as the "is" portion of a "might be" totality . . .' (Flavell, pp. 204–5). This represents a considerable achievement. Unlike all previous stages which are increasingly sophisticated means of dealing with incoming data from the environment, this stage is characterised by an ability to conjecture upon all possible events, not simply those which have occurred or are occurring, that is, by *hypothetico-deductive* reasoning. Concrete operations enable stable schemas to be formed from experience of real events. These schemas are now utilised in the formulation of *propositions*, and it is these which are the raw material of formal operations.

Formal operations closely resemble formal logical processes, or, in Piaget's view, formal logic is a symbolic representation of the highest form of thought which man achieves. Propositions can be generated by *combinatorial analysis*, a process which very clearly shows the hypothetical nature of the operations. For example, if two substances, *A* and *B*, are heated in a test tube and a gas *C* is given off, the adolescent is capable of generating hypotheses which systematically consider various contingencies based upon this observation:

    (i) *A* and *B* together produce *C*.
    (ii) *A* alone produces *C*.
    (iii) *B* alone produces *C*.
    (iv) Neither *A* nor *B* produces *C*.

Each of these is capable of empirical verification. Variables *A* and *B* can be negated by their removal, instances of reversibility.

The above example is very elementary, for variables *A* and *B* may be eliminated. Other variables are less easily handled. For instance if *A* and *B* represented the length and weight of a pendulum it would not be possible to remove either, in order to estimate its effect upon the period of swing. Instead of *negation* variables must now be held constant, or *neutralised*, in turn whilst the effects of others are investigated.

The thorough, logical procedures which epitomise the fullest achievements of formal operations can be expressed in terms of groups and lattices. Consider the possible combinations of *A* and *B* to produce gas *C*. Whereas a child using concrete operations might assume that the presence of *C* from *A* and *B* proved their joint action, the adolescent is capable of conceiving that other combinations are also true. If p represents the presence of Gas *C*, and $\bar{p}$ its absence, and q the presence of *B* and $\bar{q}$ its absence, then the following possibilities occur:

$p.q$ (Gas *C*, *B* present) $p.\bar{q}$ (Gas *C*, *B* absent)
$\bar{p}.q$ (No Gas *C*, *B* present) $\bar{p}.\bar{q}$ (No Gas *C*, *B* absent)

These combinations have not been observed, they simply exist as formal propositions which may be tested. Should further tests demonstrate that only two of these combinations exist, $(p.q)$ $(\bar{p}.\bar{q})$* this establishes the influence of substance B.

The expressions which have been used here represent combinations which can be shown to constitute a lattice, if one considers all possible arrangements of them:

1   $(p.q) \ V (p.\bar{q}) \ V (\bar{p}.q) \ V (\bar{p}.\bar{q})$
2   $p.q$
3   $p.\bar{q}$
4   $\bar{p}.q$
5   $\bar{p}.\bar{q}$
6   $(p.q) \ V (p.\bar{q})$
7   $(p.q) \ V (\bar{p}.q)$
8   $(p.q) \ V (\bar{p}.\bar{q})$
9   $(p.\bar{q}) \ V (\bar{p}.q)$
10   $(p.\bar{q}) \ V (\bar{p}.\bar{q})$
11   $(\bar{p}.q) \ V (\bar{p}.\bar{q})$
12   $(p.q) \ V (p.\bar{q}) \ V (\bar{p}.q)$
13   $(p.q) \ V (p.\bar{q}) \ V (\bar{p}.\bar{q})$
14   $(p.q) \ V (\bar{p}.q) \ V (\bar{p}.\bar{q})$
15   $(p.\bar{q}) \ V (\bar{p}.q) \ V (\bar{p}.\bar{q})$
16   $(p.q) \ V (p.\bar{q}) \ V (\bar{p}.q) \ V (\bar{p}.\bar{q})$

In addition to this lattice structure there is evidence of operations involving further characteristics of the group. A group of mathematical transformations known as the *four-group* is believed to symbolise the *structure d'ensemble* of formal operations in many problem situations.

I   (*The identity transformation*) constitutes no transformation, the proposition remains unchanged. e.g. $I(p.q) = p.q$

N   (*The negation transformation*) changes all relationships. e.g. $N(p.q) = \bar{p} \ V \ \bar{q}; N(p \ V \ q) = \bar{p}.\bar{q}$

R   (*The reciprocal transformation*) does not change conjunctions and disjunctions but transforms assertions and negations. e.g. $R(p \ V \ q) = \bar{p} \ V \ \bar{q}; R(\bar{p}.q) = p.\bar{q}$

C   (*The correlative transformation*) does not affect assertions and negations but transforms conjunctions and disjunctions. e.g. $C(p \ V \ q) = p.q; C(\bar{p}.\bar{q}) = p \ V \ q$.

These clearly constitute a group in that (i) any combination of transformations is equivalent to the implication of another;

*Note: the conjunction (.) represents 'if . . . then' e.g. $p.q.$ = if p, then q. The disjunction (V) represents 'either . . . or both' e.g. pVq = either p, or q, or both are true.

$$NC = R$$
$$N(p.q) = \bar{p} \, V \, \bar{q}$$
$$C(\bar{p} \, V \, \bar{q}) = \bar{p}.\bar{q}$$

and $R(\bar{p}.\bar{q}) = p.q$

Similarly $IN = N$, $IRC = N$, etc. This represents the rule of closure.

(ii) in accordance with the rule of associativity the ordering of sequences is unimportant, i.e. $I(RC) = (IR)C = (IC)R$

(iii) the identity element is I, and

(iv) each element can be used to transform itself into the identity element (the inverse rule), e.g. $NN=I$, $RR=I$.

It is Piaget's claim that adolescent problem-solving displays a growing facility with predictions of effects caused by negation, reciprocity, etc., not necessarily with abstract propositions but with real forces, movements, and events. The predictions which are generated are assumed to be isomorphic with the logical INRC structure, but in a physical context.

The development of these structures from those of the earlier period, that is, from groupings to these interpropositional operations involving lattices and groups, represents a widening of relatively stable, highly structured equilibrium states to even more general, abstract structures which have little dependence upon the impact of specific items of data. The example involving substances A and B, and gas C includes features which are identifiable in concrete operations. Group III, for instance, would permit of multiplication of classes of the form (A with B) + (A without B) + etc. but these would only exist in representations of actual events, not as hypotheses aimed at testing some superordinate logical structure.

Descriptions of competence in stage hierarchy

Above we have outlined Piaget's description of underlying competence at discrete points in his stage hierarchical model of development. This description raises two major problems for the empirically minded psychologist. First, how do we test 'stage' theory? What is meant by referring to a child as 'in stage X'? How do these concepts and processes manifest themselves? The second problem is how we test a theory of competence. We have said that Piaget's descriptions of the structural characteristics of each stage do not represent the performance of the behaviour at that stage but rather the underlying competence which an individual must have in order to carry out particular intellectual acts. Competence can only be manifest through particular performances, but all sorts of transient factors relating to the person, the task, and the environment can serve to impede performance. So how does one test a theory of competence? We discuss these two issues, the testing of stage theories and descriptions of competence, in Chapter 4.

The processes of development

The functional invariants

We have already alluded to the biological analogy which supposes that the principles which hold for the physical existence and development of an organism are also manifest in intellectual functioning and development. Intelligence is conceived as a special form of biological functioning which enables the creation of mental structures of increasing complexity, thus permitting a more and more effective interaction with the environment. The underlying principles which make this possible are *organisation* and *adaptation*, the functional invariants.

Adaptation to the cognitive demands of the environment has two, inter-related features. *Assimilation* is the term used to describe the process whereby a cognitive encounter with an external event results in an active processing of a representation of that event and its absorption into existing schemas (q.v.). Whilst it is often possible to construe an external event in such a way that it will 'fit' an internal schema, there are other times when this is not so, in which case the existing schemas must be reorganised to accept the new representation, a process of *accommodation*. At different times, in different circumstances, the relative degrees of assimilation and accommodation will vary, but it is sensible only to think of them as functioning in an inter-related fashion. In the most elementary act of adding our construction of a novel event to an existing schema, we are, in fact changing that schema; and the demand to restructure an existing schema may be generated from a need to assimilate a novel event, or from an internal need for spontaneous reconstruction.

These twin processes which make up adaptation represent the dynamic aspects of a cognitive system. Their orderly functioning presumes some lawful system or *organisation*. Exactly how the cognitive system will be set up will differ from time to time, but it will never be random and never chaotic. The totality of the system is integrated, and no change takes place without repercussions throughout all its parts.

Figurative and operative knowledge

Piaget makes a distinction between knowledge as content (figurative knowledge), and knowledge as process (operative knowledge). In the last analysis thinking processes cannot be used without content, hence the distinction is essentially one of emphasis; but the conception of the difference helps us to focus on what is general and mobile in thought, as opposed to what is specific and particular. Furth (1977) explains the distinction in this way: 'one could say that the figurative aspect deals with what is usually called the "observable", whereas the operative aspect is that which has to be inferred' (p. 67). Thus figurative and operative knowledge are not different kinds of knowledge, but are different ways of looking at the same knowledge.

The distinction poses some problems. For example, one cannot define *a priori* what is observable and what is to be inferred. What is observed is a function of what the observer already knows.

However problematic, the distinction is of considerable importance in Piaget's theory. The origins of figurative knowledge are in perception and imitation, whilst operative knowledge arises from internal feedback as a consequence of the person's own interaction with the environment. 'Understanding (i.e. operative knowledge) is never observed in the outside world, it is always an operative feedback from the person's own activity. So the source of figurative knowing is the outside world, whereas the source of operative knowing is the child's own activity on the outside world' (Furth, 1977, p. 70).

Schemas

The term *schema* has already been introduced, as a means of referring to the representations of an event existing within the individual. However, Piaget's use of the term is misrepresented by such a simple explanation, and it is important to investigate his meaning in rather more detail.

Schemas are usually referred to by the behavioural patterns with which they are associated, e.g. a *schema of sucking* in early childhood; but by labelling it in this way Piaget is implying that something underlies the overt behaviour. The implication is that the complex of related aspects of the act have been organised into a relatively stable cognitive structure which operates as a total entity. Although individual acts of sucking may vary slightly, as in sucking a lollipop or a nipple, the overall schema remains the same, representing a class of acts with common features, and the activation of one aspect of it is not possible without the activation of all other parts.

In spite of this seemingly static description, it is a highly flexible entity, capable of rapid changes as the processes of assimilation and accommodation operate upon it. Furthermore, schemas represent an incredibly diverse range of human experiences, from sucking to complex problem solving, from prehension to sight. Once established, a schema will be operated on every occasion in which seemingly appropriate aspects of the environment present themselves; in other words, the interaction with the environment is self-motivated.

The dynamics of change—equilibration

Having examined the genetic predispositions which make cognitive development possible (the functional invariants), and also the basic organisation of internal representations (schemas), it remains to find the driving force which dictates that change will occur. In order for each cognitive structure to be refined and to be superseded by another, presumably more efficient structure, some mechanism has to be capable of deriving alternative cognitive structures from experience. This mechanism is energised by the *principle of equilibrium* and the process of *equilibration*. The concept of equilibrium being employed here is that of dynamic constructive equilibrium.

In interaction with the environment the organism attempts to create a balance between the processes of assimilation and accommodation. This process of equilibration gives rise to transient equilibrium states in which the cognitive relationship between the organism and the external event is relatively stable. Yet the very nature of the schemas so derived, that is, their constant application to other situations, drives them again into disequilibrium.

Equilibrium states exist for every manifestation of cognition. Some accommodate and assimilate widely divergent objects or events, such as the groupings of concrete operations. Others are much more restricted in scope. This capacity is referred to as the *field of application.*

It is also possible to discriminate between equilibrium states in terms of their *mobility.* This refers to the effectiveness with which an equilibrium state can be transferred from one datum to another. This transfer may occur between two or more precepts, concepts, or actions; or it may move between modalities.

Furthermore, equilibrium states admit of different degrees of *stability.* Just as a pilot's facility to counteract fluctuations is probably superior to that of the yachtsman because of the means at his disposal, so certain states more readily cope with the disturbing effects of experiential data than others. Specifically, the equilibrium states of perceptual and pre-operational action have limited stability. They are relatively easily overcome by vagaries of the perceptual apparatus such as illusion. Operational states, on the other hand, are more stable. The operation of reversibility, for instance, ensures an entirely equilibrated system which deals effectively with what was previously perturbing in certain transformations of data presented.

These characteristics identify differing degrees of efficiency within equilibrium states, some being more efficient than others. In consequence, the general model has a clear logical direction to it. Cognitive development involves progression through a series of equilibrium states towards those which offer the greatest field of application, or degree of mobility and stability.

Piaget has attempted to describe the actual process of equilibration in some detail by reference to the acquisition of conservation (Piaget, 1957a). The experiment employed the apparent transformation of a volume of liquid by pouring it into a container of different dimensions. In Piaget's view successful treatment of the display requires that the child be able to compensate for changes in liquid level by related changes in the width, or cross-section, of the vessel.

At the pre-operational stage the child is thought to have an equilibrated structure which is based purely upon the appearance of one particular feature. That is, he will confidently state that, as the level of the liquid has changed, there is more or less liquid.

Subsequently this equilibrium state appears to break down, as the child's judgments become less confident. Piaget maintains that the child begins to perceive other aspects of the situation which may not be assimilated into the pre-conceptual schema. Attempts to encompass them lead to a fundamental re-organisation of structure.

Analysis suggested four steps in the process. In the first of these the child attends to only one attribute, perhaps the height. Changes in height are then interpreted as equivalent changes in quantity. In the second step the child becomes aware of a second variable, and may transfer attention to that as the sole relevant attribute. Step three includes a variety of behaviours which are unified by apprehension of both attributes within a single cognitive act. Then in step 4 a clear act of conservation is produced, in which the child successfully compensates for variations in one attribute by variations in the other.

Concurrent with the later steps is the emergence of the logical notion that, as nothing has been added to, or taken from the liquid it must still be the same quantity. This principle, which provides a logical basis for the compensations, is known as the Principle of Invariance.

However, the general process of equilibration is purported to underlie all cognitive development, and whilst the four steps may appear with reasonable clarity in the experiment cited, or others of similar type, it is not certain that they may be discerned in experiments using perceptual or sensori-motor tasks. For this reason Pinard and Laurendeau (1969) argue that 'it seems better to liberalize the pattern a bit by disregarding those of its elements that are too specific or limited to a particular type of cognitive structure' (p. 152). They then produce a general formula, that the evolution of behaviour within any cognitive sector is characterised by the progressive coordination of actions (overt or interiorized) that are at first isolated one from another and centered on the results produced each time, rather than on the changes that link these results (p. 152).

Thus the detail of equilibration consists of successive decentrings which affect the extent to which subsequent actions can encompass greater degrees of variability, or more extensive transformations.

Piaget's model of the dynamics of cognitive growth emphasises the interaction between ongoing structures and the external environment. It represents his attempt to avoid the limitations of both empiricism and rationalism or *a priorism*. Empiricism holds that we are given items of information in experience. Development on this basis must be independent of any necessary ordering of experience or structure. Indeed Piaget describes empiricism as 'geneticism without structure'. In rationalism the view is taken that experience conforms from the beginning to the structure that thought determines. Experience has to be fitted into what is given in thought. Piaget refers to this view as 'structuralism without genesis'; that is to say that there is no real development. In Piaget's view there is a dynamic and constructivist interaction between experience and ongoing structures. But precisely what form does this interaction take? If the impact of experience is limited by structural characteristics what are these limits? If the sequence of development is necessary and ordered then it seems that all 'experience' can do is to provide energy to alter the rate of development. It cannot provide 'information' to alter structural characteristics.

Piaget's view of equilibration is highly abstract. How can it be evaluated? At what points do the terms used in describing equilibration actually come into contact with data? What testable predictions can be generated from this account? An appraisal of Piaget's view of learning (i.e. the impact of experience) and the development of cognition is left to Chapter 5.

Summary

We have described Piaget's view of the epigenetic nature of cognitive development. He postulates a necessary (i.e. causally related) sequence of stages. The contents of each stage are described as structural isomorphs of logico-mathematical domains, and we have argued that these descriptions represent the competence necessary to fulfil the performance characteristics of a given stage. The process of development involves a structurally dominated but constructive interaction with the environment. To evaluate such a view of cognitive growth we have stated that it is necessary to explore further the problems in conceptualising and empirically testing the notion of stage, the competence/performance distinction and the equilibrium model. These we do in subsequent chapters.

Chapter 3

Problems in validating the theory

We have already noted that scientific theories must be intimately related to empirical data. Theories must have their roots in data, but the whole of a theory is not so embedded; we expect to be able to use theories to predict data we have not yet got. Thus, when asking questions about the validity of a theory we are asking about the relationship between the theory and the data it claims to account for.

Does the theory give a clear and unambiguous account of the data used in its support? Is the theory the only account we have of this data or are there competing accounts using different theoretical terms and relationships? If there are competing accounts how do the competitors perform when put to critical test? With respect to predictive validity, what testable statements are made from the theory and how far do these match data subsequently gathered?

It is possible to examine Piaget's theory with respect to each of these kinds of question. For our purpose we have chosen specific examples of relevant work to illustrate the conceptual and methodological problems involved in critically appraising the edifice Piaget has constructed. It is our view that some important critical work is available and it has much to say about the validity of the Genevan theory.

In particular in what follows we look at the concurrent validity of the theory by discussing studies which offer alternative accounts of some of Piaget's work on pre-operational thought. With respect to predictive validity, some of the more general claims of the theory (for example the claim of universal sequence of stages) are explored in the light of the studies from cross-cultural psychology.

It will become clear that assessing the validity of a theory is a complex undertaking involving inter-related conceptual and methodological problems. Our concern here is to appraise these general problems as well as to make comment on Piaget's theory.

Concurrent validity

One great strength of Piaget's theory is that it raises a huge number of interesting questions. In exploring these questions a massive amount of data has been collected. Piaget makes a large number of claims about the intellectual limitations of children. These claims are based on the data gathered by Piaget and his colleagues and are presented as explanations of this data. Piaget claims, for example, that children fail transitive inference tasks because they cannot handle propositional logic. That they fail the tasks is an observation: that they cannot handle propositional logic is an explanation of that observation. It is an explanation of particular observations and the explanation itself is consistent with, and part of, a more general explanation, i.e. the theory of intellectual development. Piaget also claims that infant school children do not possess the concept of conservation and that they are (intellectually) egocentric in that they cannot imagine points of view other than their own. Additionally, he claims that babies lack object constancy; that is they do not realise that objects have an existence independent of their actions on the objects. It must be emphasised that a lack of object constancy or conservations or the prevalence of egocentricity are not observations but explanations of observations. Each of Piaget's separate accounts is part of a general account of the development of a mental apparatus which can be described in terms of the logical structures outlined in the previous chapters.

In almost all cases, Piaget's critics accept his observations. They assert however, that there are alternative explanations of these observations. They further claim that these alternative explanations have never been eliminated by Piagetians, that the alternatives are more testable and that on testing they fit the data better than the Genevan theory (Siegel and Brainerd, 1978).

We have no intention of surveying all these data here. It is however, useful to illustrate some general points. Piaget claims that pre-school children cannot conserve number or quantity of material. Transformations of arrays involving change of shape or distribution are judged to alter the child's estimate of quantity. However, it has been shown that children as young as three years do conserve number in the face of such transformations if the set size involved is of the order of two or three units (Gelman, 1972, 1977; Gelman and Tucker, 1975). If the ability to conserve depends on set size it raises the question of what it means to judge someone a conserver or non-conserver. Additionally, it has been shown that five-year-olds conserve quantity providing they are required to make only one judgment (i.e. following the transformation) rather than two judgments (one before and one after transformation) (Rose and Blank, 1974). This raises the question of the role of the child's interpretation of the contextual cues involved in testing him. Piaget's account of infantile absence of object constancy is based on observation of infants' search behaviours. However, Bower (1974) has shown that, with more sensitive response measures, babies do appear to exhibit behaviour which implies object constancy and Cornell (1978) suggests that Piaget's observations are artefacts of the reinforcement contingencies manifest in his object permanence tests. The three general points here are (i) that if we wish to establish the absence or presence of a particular operation we need tasks which require the use of that and only that operation and which can be done in no other way, (ii) that the operation (which is a construct of the experimenter) must not be occluded by response limitations on the part of the child, i.e. we need to give tasks such that the physical limitations of the child do not prevent his showing his intellectual capacity, (iii) the task context has to be designed in such a way that we do not generate artefactual behaviours, i.e. that we do not 'lead the child on'.

These are excruciatingly difficult requirements to place on the design of experiments. They are not merely practical problems of experimental design however. They raise issues about how we conceptualise intellectual processes and their acquisition, about how we assess mental contents, about the impact of theory on observation and vice versa and about the way science progresses in accumulating theory. Rather than exhaustively surveying data on object constancy, egocentricity or conservation, in what follows we examine one important debate in detail with a view to appraising the Piagetian stance on these more general problems. For this purpose we focus on Piaget's claim regarding the operational immaturity of pre-operational children as it manifests itself in their performance on tasks requiring transitive inference.

The great transitive-inference show

Suppose we have three sticks, the longest being red, the medium one blue, and the shortest yellow. Suppose also, these are hidden from the view of a child we wish to study. We show him the red and the blue stick and ask for his judgment of the longer of the two sticks. We show him the blue and the yellow stick and ask for a similar judgment. These judgments are based on what he can see and responses from three-year-olds upwards concur with adult judgments. Now, without showing the child the sticks any further we ask him which is the longer, the red or the yellow stick. This judgment cannot be based on immediate perception. The judgments of children from seven years upwards agree with those of adults. Children of four or five and many six-year-olds, respond randomly to such tasks; they are as likely to nominate the yellow stick as the red one. The observation that older children respond more like adults than younger children is uninteresting. The interesting question is why young children respond in this way and how they come to respond like us. It becomes particularly important to our endeavour since this task is a significant one in respect of Piaget's theory. Piaget's theory explains the development of cognition in terms of the acquisition of intellectual processes isomorphic with logical processes. Additionally, his interpretation of the young child's failure on this task is based on three assumptions. First, the task demands the logical process of transitive inference. Second, adults do the task by applying such a process, and third, the young child's failure is because he does not possess that logical mechanism. Young children's performance on this task is taken to exemplify their intellectual inadequacies in this respect (Piaget, 1953, 1970b).

The Piagetian case is open to question on all three of the above counts. First, it is entirely possible that whilst such a task can be done via a process of transitive inference, it need not necessarily be done so. It could be done, for example, by building a picture in one's memory of the three sticks and their relative dimensions. Second, it is entirely possible that adults do the task in exactly such a way. Third, young children could fail the task for many reasons other than those based on logical immaturity. It could be that they do not understand the question we ask them, or they have not remembered the information on which such a task can be solved, or that they did not take in the information in the first place. Each of these reasons for failure is, in itself, complex and question begging. To say that young children do not understand questions or do not take in information or cannot remember information they have taken in leaves us with the problem of accounting for these limitations. The point is, however, that unless these alternative hypotheses concerning failure on this task are ruled out, we cannot securely maintain that children lack logical mechanisms. Bryant and Trabasso (1971) were first responsible for testing this kind of criticism of Piaget's work although the general ambiguity of interpretation had been noted long before their publication (Braine, 1964; Smedslund, 1965).

Bryant's work set out to re-raise the question, 'can preschool children make transitive inferences?' A vigorous debate has ensued which has far reaching implications for Piaget's theory. Bryant's initial point was that if we want to claim that children fail problems because of an underlying logical incompetence then we must rule out other possible explanations of failure. He suggested that young children fail transitive inference problems because they forget the propositions on which they would have to base the inference. Bryant's second point was that asking a child to make an inference across three quantities is not enough to ensure that he must do the problem by inference. If a child is told $A > B$ and $B > C$ he might conclude (correctly) $A > C$ because he remembers the initial labels (i.e. A is bigger than, C is smaller than) from the initial comparisons. Bryant thus trained children on four comparisons across five quantities ($A > B$, $B > C$, $C > D$ and $D > E$). The test required the child to make a comparison between B and D. Since B and D have both 'bigger than' and 'smaller than' labels in training, parroting initial labels would be unhelpful.

In two experiments (Bryant and Trabasso, 1971) these two variables were taken into account. Children learned the four basic comparisons and their memories were checked before making the test comparison. It was possible to show that four-year-olds answered this comparison correctly at well above chance level. Bryant and Trabasso's results have been confirmed by Roodin and Gruen (1970) and by de Boysson-Bardies and O'Regan (1973). The latter, however, reject Bryant's interpretation of the findings. They were concerned to point out that not only must we eliminate other possible accounts of failure, we must also ensure that when children are successful they are successful by no other process except transitive inference.

De Boysson-Bardies and O'Regan replicated Bryant and Trabasso's study. Children were presented with the four comparisons in ascending or descending order (i.e. $A > B$; $B > C$; $C > D$; $D > E$ or $E < D$; $D < C$; $C < B$; $B < A$). They were trained with one pair at a time until they made 8 to 10 correct judgments and then they moved on to the next pair. After that, the four pairs were presented in random order until on each pair the child made two successive, correct responses. (Bryant and Trabasso demanded six successive, correct responses.) Scores on testing the relationship between B and D were compatible with Bryant and Trabasso's. However, the authors noted an intriguing difference. They used a lesser learning criterion (2 instead of 6 successive correct answers) and their children did just as well on the unlearned (transitive inference) comparison as Bryant's. Yet they did, predictably, less well on the learned comparisons. If they were doing less well on the learning, on what basis were they solving the inference problem? Could it be that the children had strategies other than transitive inference on which to base their judgment? Recall that the training occurred in ascending or descending order. As a consequence it is possible that the child had only to remember which of the to-be-compared sticks were shown first. In a second study therefore, de Boysson-Bardies and O'Regan presented the training pairs randomly to a group of adults and a group of children of mean age 4.3 years. The children did no worse in this 'disorder' condition than they did in the ordered condition but the adults did significantly worse and somewhat worse than the children. The perplexed authors concluded that either 'children implement transitivity differently and sometimes better than adults . . . (or) . . . that children were not using transitivity at all' (de Boysson-Bardies and O'Regan, 1973, p. 533).

As an alternative they suggested that the young children might be using an 'end point labelling' strategy. It was argued that the child recognises that A is always the big end point and E is always the small end point. They are also assumed to notice that A is always associated with B and therefore make B large by association. In a similar way D becomes small by association with E. Thus when asked to compare B and D they judge B large and D small therefore $B > D$. Bryant has noted that, 'this is such a complex train of thought that it is difficult to believe that any child who can manage it cannot also manage an inference' (Bryant, 1977, p. 62), but he recognises that it is an alternative he did not rule out.

Three studies of end point labelling strategies are available. In their initial paper de Boysson-Bardies and O'Regan presented children with only two pairs of sticks $A > B$ and $C > D$. The children had no way of knowing the relationships A, D or B,C. On a labelling hypothesis A and C would be labelled 'big' and B and D 'small'. Consequently we would expect the judgments $A > D$ and $C > B$. These, in fact, were the judgments that the children tended to give. The authors suggest that, as an alternative expectation,

> a young child possessing a notion of transitivity or using any kind of 'ordering method' would impose an order on a set of sticks even when there is insufficient information to know the correct order. . . . Thus in this experiment, the most obvious thing for him to assume is either that $A > B > C > D$ or else that $C > D > A > B$. Under this hypothesis then, and in contrast to the 'labelling' hypothesis, if the child chooses $A > D$ he should make $B > C$. (de Boysson-Bardies and O'Regan, 1973, p. 534.)

Whilst the data support the authors' contention that children have strategies other than transitive inference the relevance of this study to Bryant's experiment is difficult to see. De Boysson-Bardies and O'Regan suggest that given that we inform the child $A > B$ and $C > D$ then his construal of $A/C > B/D$ may be called labelling and is likely whilst his construal $A > B > C > D$ may be called 'ordering' and is unlikely. It would seen *under these givens* that the child 'labels'. But given this limited amount of data this might be all he can do and it says nothing about what he does when given more data.

In any event, contradictory evidence has been produced by Harris and Bassett (1975). In their first experiment they used the typical method of coloured sticks with no visual feedback. The four sticks represented the quantities $A = B > C = D$. They hypothesised that if children adopt end point labels then A and D would be labelled 'same' and hence judged equal. Their four-year-old children, however, correctly concluded that $A > D$. If nothing else this study suggests what an exceedingly strange strategy end point labelling is when reduced to this absurd context. Harris and Bassett's second experiment was rather more convincing. The propositions 'Peter is the same size as David, David is bigger than you, you are the same size as John' were given to four-year-old children four times. They were then asked the relationship between Peter and John. 19/26 children correctly concluded that Peter was bigger than John. This result detracts from Piaget's view and supports Bryant's contention providing we assume for the moment that the problem is actually solved using a process of transitive inference.

Bryant (1977) reports a similar experiment of his own. He gave four-year-old children comparisons of the form $A > B$ and $Y > Z$. Coloured sticks were used and the children never saw their complete lengths. Half the children were simply told $A > B$ and $Y > Z$. The rest were taught that A was the longest and Z the shortest of all four sticks, i.e. they were given end point training. They were then asked to compare B and Y. If this end point labelling hypothesis were correct then the second group should judge $B > Y$ more often than the first group. In fact there was no difference between the two groups and no evidence that either of them thought that B was longer than Y.

It is Bryant's judgment that the evidence supports the contention that young children can take transitive inferences and that 'no one has been able to produce one single instance of a child who can remember the information essential for an inference, but cannot combine it inferentially' (Bryant, 1977, p. 62).

However we now do have evidence that children can

remember propositions and yet do not combine them inferentially and there is evidence that when they do combine propositions to produce correct solutions, the combination is not necessarily based on inferential processes.

In a study by Halford and Galloway (1977) 163 children whose ages ranged from four-and-a-half to nine years were presented with three rods in two pairs. A blue rod (65 cm long) and a yellow rod (64 cm) were placed alongside each other and the child decided which was the longer. The yellow rod was then compared in a similar way with a red rod (63 cm long). The yellow rod was removed and the red and blue rods were placed on a table at right angles to each other. Thus the famous horizontal-vertical illusion was used to make the red rod appear longer. They were then asked which was the longer. Since the longer (blue) rod would not appear so, it would be judged longer only on the basis of logical necessity. The children were then tested for their recall of the original comparisons. The important result here was that 87 children (i.e. 54 per cent of the sample) recalled both comparisons but did not make the transitive inference judgment. It seems that failure on this task is not wholly due to memory limits. Halford and Galloway contend that the intensive training procedures used by Bryant and his colleagues allow children to solve the problems by processes other than transitive inference. Since they do not offer a suggestion as to what these other strategies might be the whole problem of what we mean by transitivity comes to the forefront. It is clear that in attempts to control for alternative accounts of both success and failure on transitivity tasks a wide range of experimental procedures has been generated and it might be that the precise nature of Piaget's claim has been lost from view.

Piaget's view of all logical operations is that for a child to 'possess' such a process it must be 'operational'. In Halford and Galloway's words,

> much of the confusion in the literature seems to result from failure to ensure that tasks designed to measure transitivity do in fact reflect the child's understanding of the necessity of this association. A procedure which merely tests knowledge of specific instances, as Bryant and Trabasso's procedure appears to do, cannot determine whether a child has transitivity (1977, p. 4).

It is implied in this view that Bryant and Trabasso have an elemental view of transitivity and that this is inappropriate to testing Piaget's 'operational' view. Unfortunately, the 'operational' view requires that processes be used in a co-ordinated manner and linked to a whole structure or system of other operations. This makes the view extremely difficult to test. Conceptual and procedural problems are created.

Conceptually, it makes difficulties for the study of the acquisition of operational competence. It seems unlikely that a mechanism such as transitive inference would appear in the first instance in its full operational form and if this is the case what are its precursors? If we agree that 'knowledge of specific instances' does not test operativity we might still claim that it tells us something about children's inferential competence in its early stages. Claiming that the presence of transitive inference must be ascertained in all its operational complexity begs the question of how we construe the acquisition of this process.

Procedurally, tests of operational transitivity as opposed to elemental transitivity are necessarily indirect and complex. Halford's method for example deliberately juxtaposes a well known illusion effect with a demand for logical necessity. How many adults would have their reason strained by con-flicting demands presented by a high status figure who appeared trustworthy? As Flavell has noted in reference to the use of illusions to challenge operational knowledge,

> The child may also not entertain the possibility that the adult experimenter could be deceiving him, although this is, of course, exactly what the authority figure is doing. . . . You might not entertain it either, if the Pope or George Washington were testing you (1977, p. 225).

On this basis the child might have a perfectly good grasp of transitive inference and yet set it aside because of the contex-tual demands of the task. More trivially he might be answer-ing the question 'which stick looks longer?' as opposed to the question 'which stick is longer?'

To summarise the argument so far, the Genevans claim that an important limitation of the preconceptual thinker is that he cannot combine propositions in an inferential manner. Critics agree that young children fail on Piagetian tests of transitive inference but believe that there are alternative accounts of this failure. When they control for these processes young children do succeed on such tasks. In response the Genevans argue that when children do succeed they are likely to be using processes which are not inferential and in any event non-Piagetian tests of transitive inference are not testing for operational inference at all. Only tests which demand a demonstration of the child's grasp of the logical necessity of the conclusion based on inference are considered pertinent. Finally, we have seen that such tasks are typically complex and indirect, that they demand perceptual, linguistic, and memory resources as well as logical competence and as a consequence will always be open to multiple interpretations. Additionally, the demand that we search for full-blown, operational transitivity seems strange from developmental theorists since no account is then given of how we spot the precursors of transitivity if indeed any precursors are envisaged. It looks like a stalemate; if we accept Piaget's claim and endeavour to test it we need an unambiguous test of operational transitivity, but the notion of 'operational' is so embedded in other processes that such a test seems unlikely to be produced.

This impasse can be avoided by returning to the original claim, because the fact is that whilst the term 'transitive inference' adequately describes a kind of logical problem there is no account provided by Piaget of what it involves as a psychological process. There is no description given of how children or adults actually *do* these problems, i.e. there is nothing said about the contents and sequence of procedures involved in solving these tasks. Piaget makes the claim that adults solve such problems by inferential means and that pre-operational children cannot because they lack the inferential means. He provides no process account of what goes on in someone's head when solving such a problem. If we knew more about the actual processes involved in these tasks we would not need to look for an unambiguous test of whether someone 'has' transitive inference or not. Rather, we would seek to understand *how* they did a particular problem. Now this represents a very different view of how to make progress with this problem than the one adopted by previous researchers in this field. It has been concluded that in the search for tests of the possession of operations, such requirements beg the question in so far as theory is concerned. That is, one assumes the theory to be true and then devises tests that purport to show its presence or absence. Our view is that science is inductive and we prefer to infer the mechanisms underlying the behaviour from empirical evidence (Riley and Trabasso, 1974, p. 201).

To re-state this point, Riley and Trabasso are claiming that it makes more sense to try to identify cognitive processes from the study of empirical evidence rather than to search for the presence or absence of constructs (like transitive inference) which have been derived from a logic-model of intellectual development and which have never been specified in psychological terms.

Trabasso and his colleagues have made an impressive start to the study of transitive inference as a psychological process (Riley and Trabasso, 1974; Trabasso, 1975; 1977). Their work is complex. Typically it involves teaching subjects the relationship between pairs of quantities from a series and then asking them to answer questions about the series. The time taken to answer these questions is measured and the number of trials to learn particular relationships is recorded. These data are then used to explore various models of the intellectual processes and contents used in reaching solutions. Their data suggest that subjects gradually construct an image-like representation of the series presented. When they are asked a question about pairs in the array they appear not to operate a step by step, logical sequence but to read out from their image. These processes seem to be at work whether the subject is four years or twenty years of age. The developmental difference seems to be merely that the younger the child, the more trials he needs to build his representation of the series. The manner of the building and the mode and success of its use are independent of age.

Trabasso concludes that

We believe that our research provides strong evidence that Piaget (is) . . . not correct. The age and performance correlation disappears when one makes sure that the child understands and can remember the information critical to making inferences. If so, there seems to be no clear sequence in emergence of such abilities. The logic model, while a reasonable description of task structures and task dependency does not seem to be a very good psychological model (Trabasso, 1977, p. 365).

However, this conclusion must be interpreted in the light of criticisms of Trabasso's work (see Chapter 4).

The impact of theory on research

Piaget claims that pre-school children lack the capacity to make operational transitive inferences. Some of his critics disagree. In reviewing some of the earlier work related to this debate we showed that something of an impasse was reached. The debate seemed to hinge on finding a test for the possession of transitive inference, the results of which could be interpreted unambiguously. Certain propositions seemed to have been taken for granted by the parties to this debate. First, they assumed that the processes of inference could in some way be isolated from perceptual, linguistic and memory processes. It seems highly unlikely that such pure and unitary processes exist. Attempts to take such an atomistic approach to cognitive acts may be misleading. Second, it seems to have been assumed that Piaget had offered a description of a psychological process. In fact he has done no such thing. Rather, he has pointed to the structure of a task. Finally, it seems to have been taken as self-evident that the mature thinker uses this process whilst the pre-operational thinker cannot. No data demanded this distinction because Piaget offered no data about *how* people solved or failed his problems. Rather his *theory* demanded this distinction since it arises out of characterising intellectual development in terms of a logic model. Some of those testing the claim, operating in a hypothetico-deductive fashion seem to have been blinkered by these assumptions. They were assuming the theory to be true in order to develop the machinery to test it.

Trabasso and his colleagues have avoided the above assumptions by asking, '*how* do people solve these problems?' Their data show that in so far as Piaget makes remarks about the process limitations of young children he is wrong. Trabasso concludes, 'For the most part, we have found that children can, in fact, reason like adults. Adults, in turn, seem to employ reasoning strategies like children' (Trabasso, 1977, p. 365).

Predictive validity

> Psychology elaborated in our environment, which is charac-
> terised by a certain culture and a certain language, remains
> essentially conjectural as long as the necessary cross-
> cultural material has not been gathered as a control (J.
> Piaget, 1976, p. 268).

Piaget makes a number of claims and conjectures which take
the theory far beyond the limited data on which it was based.
It is claimed that the structure and sequence of the stages of
development are universal, that is they are expected to be
found in all children regardless of cultural background. It is
further speculated that, regardless of culture, the route to
cognitive acquisitions (e.g. the development of conservation)
is the same. This is not to say that it is claimed that specific
cultural experiences make no difference. Speculation on the
role of experience is extensive and it is recognised that it is
at the heart of different *rates* of development. It is only the
routes and landmarks which are reckoned to be universal. The
speculative nature of these claims is recognised and the role
of cross-cultural studies in assessing their validity is clearly
spelt out.

> We have considered it possible to recognise these character-
> istics in the development of the operations and the logico-
> mathematical structures of intelligence. If this is so, it
> would naturally mean a certain constancy or uniformity in
> development, whatever the social environments in which
> individuals live. On the other hand, inversions in the suc-
> cession of stages, or major modification of their character-
> istics, from one milieu to another, would mean that these
> basic biological factors do not intervene in the cognitive
> development of individuals. This is the first fundamental
> problem, the solution of which requires extensive cross-
> cultural studies (J. Piaget, 1976, p. 260).

In attempting to assess this kind of claim recourse to the
study of other cultures is essential. A diversity of physical,
social and religious experience underpins an exciting range of
occupations, preoccupations, practices and modes of expression of intellectual processes. It is possible to study performance on psychological tasks as we move from groups who

have been schooled to groups unschooled, from urban to rural environments, from one class or caste group to another, from nomads to farmers and from technological to 'primitive' societies. Psychologists have taken their tests and problems from African scrub to South American rain forests and from the deserts of Australia to Arctic wastelands in their attempts to explore the relationship between societal provision of experience and the development of cognition.

Unfortunately, making sense of this natural laboratory is not without its difficulties. If we endeavour to study natural, everyday activities in a variety of societies with a view to identifying the underlying intellectual processes used, we are faced with the problem of making unambiguous inferences from what we see. In hunting fish, does the Eskimo make a series of deductions based on clues regarding ice thickness, gull flocks and the like? Or is he simply following tribal habits which lead him to believe that there are always fish at point X? The second problem is that without some degree of control (in an experimental sense) in our observations it would be impossible either to estimate the relevance of any particular experience to any particular intellectual skill or to make meaningful comparisons between various cultural groups. Without some baseline of comparison it is likely that we would be overwhelmed by the very cultural diversity which attracted us in the first place and to emphasise in our conclusions cross-cultural differences rather than transcultural commonalities.

An alternative strategy to ethnographic observation is to take standard tasks or problems to a variety of tribes which differ along a specifiable dimension (for example, the degree to which their children are schooled). We would then attempt to relate task performance to this independent variable.

Sadly, as Labov (1970) has pointed out, 'formal experimental equivalence does not ensure equal experimental treatment for members of different cultural groups'. Some groups might be more or less familiar with the task or more or less impressed by its significance or more or less threatened by the testing situation. In attempts to meet these problems, psychologists have endeavoured to design 'culture fair' tasks or tests. In general this involves producing material equally novel and strange to each culture and hence artificial to all. This artificiality causes us to question the significance or the validity of the findings of such studies.

Clearly, using cross-cultural research to explore the role of experience leaves us with something of a dilemma. Standardised tasks are seen as artificial and lacking in significance whilst natural behaviour sequences are ambiguous and open to a variety of interpretations. If it is possible, what is needed to break out of this dilemma is the identification of intellectual skills of universal significance and the design of a methodology to assess their development. The Genevans lay claim to just such a body of work. More important than this the work is claimed to be located within a coherent scientific framework.

Specifically, in Piaget's theory the processes of intelligence at the heart of intellectual development are, by definition, biologically universal, i.e. common to all humans. Second, the hierarchical sequence of development and the intellectual structures developed to deal with varying mental contents said to have been discovered in Swiss children are also claimed to be universal (Piaget, 1950, Piaget and Inhelder, 1969). Thus whilst interactive experience is clearly recognised as essential to development (Piaget and Inhelder, 1967) and to influence to some degree the *rate* of development, both the structures and the sequence in which they are acquired are said to be universal. Additionally, the structures identified as marking this development are not trivial. Piaget considers conservation to be 'a necessary condition for all rational activity' (Piaget and Szeminska, 1952, p. 3).

Thus it has been claimed that Piaget's contribution to cross-cultural psychology has been the identification of significant skills, the proposition of a model of how the skills are put together and the development of a fine grain methodology by which these claims can be explored (Goodnow, 1969a). Certainly these claims have initiated a prodigious body of research.

The popularity of Piaget's account of intellectual development in children has generated the single largest body of related research in the area of cross-cultural studies (Cole and Scribner, 1974, p. 29).

Perhaps in no other area of psychology is there so much cross-cultural and cross-social class empirical research data available as in the Piagetian tasks (Modgil, 1974, p. 226).

Cross-cultural contributions to validation of the theory

It is not our task here to report or review all this work. (For extensive reviews see Ashton, 1975; Dasen, 1972; Goodnow, 1969b; Modgil, 1974; Modgil and Modgil, 1976.) Our concern is not with the contribution that Piaget has made to cross-cultural psychology (although the general conclusion that the results are irregular or difficult to interpret (Vernon, 1976; Modgil, 1974) would suggest that results are not fulfilling expectations). Rather we are concerned with whether the data obtained throw light on the claims of the theory. Is the postulated sequence of development universal? Is there a coherent universal structure amongst operations in a given stage? What is the significance of the acquisitions identified by Piaget? What can we say about the role of experience in the development of intellectual skills? What useful contribution has been made to the comprehension of epigenetic processes?

The issues raised by these questions are inter-related in complex ways. In the following sections we discuss each in turn and then comment on the general implications of our remarks. First we must repeat that there is a vast literature on cross-cultural studies and we are not attempting an exhaustive review. Indeed our attention will focus on what is irregular, confusing and critical. In turning from the consistent and focusing on the incongruent we are in no way being 'unfair' to the theory. In fact we are indulging in Piaget's famous epigenetic process of equilibration. We are more likely to develop advanced and general structures (theories) by resolving inconsistencies than by dwelling on the familiar and congruent.

Is the Piagetian developmental sequence universal?

A number of studies have confirmed that in general, children in a wide range of cultures pass through the stages and the within-stage sequences which Piaget described for Swiss children (Elkind, 1961; Hyde, 1959; Lovell 1961; Mohseni, 1966; Price-Williams, 1961; Prince, 1968; for example). However, there are enough irregularities in the studies to cause concern and make interpretation ambiguous. The conclusions based on the above studies always relate to the general or average trend of test performance.

In many studies there are numerous children whose performance does not conform to the perfect Guttman scale which one would expect. Hyde (1959) for example, showed that whilst the general trend of her data was consistent with the Genevan sequence, some Arab and Somali children conserved weight but not quantity whereas Piaget's results show that conservation of quantity precedes conservation of weight. For some children then the developmental sequence seems to have been disturbed. There are alternative interpretations however. It could be that they were more or less familiar with some of the subtests; it could be, quite simply, a case of performance variability due to loss of attention, fatigue or a temporarily confusing question. Thus we do not know for these children whether the development sequence is disturbed or whether we have cases of measurement error. In reporting the general trend of these results the authors are ignoring alternative accounts and assuming measurement error to be at the root of irregular performance.

There are more impressive demonstrations of 'non-Genevan' sequence than the above however. There are studies in which the general trend of performance has run counter to Piaget's findings. For example, Boonsong (1968) found a simultaneous development of the conservation of quantity and weight in her children. Similar order discrepancies have been reported by Dasen (1970), De Lemos (1966) and Bovet (1974). In Bovet's study, Algerian children of eight to nine years were found to be *less* advanced than their peers of seven to eight on tests of conservation of continuous quantity.

These discrepancies are serious. They conflict not only with Genevan observations, 'The concepts of conservation are acquired in a constant chronological order' (Inhelder, Sinclair, and Bovet, 1974, p. 246) but also with the claim to the generality of this finding: 'Studies undertaken in Geneva and by other researchers in various countries confirm this order' (ibid.) and it makes problematic the claim that, with respect to conservation concepts; '. . . their growth is governed by very regular laws of development' (ibid., p. 32).

It is important to stress that Piaget's theory does not postulate a *necessary* order for these acquisitions. Rather an empirically well established, lawful order is claimed. Thus these discrepant studies demand some reconceptualisation of this lawfulness or must be shown to be at odds on methodological grounds.

For example, Brainerd (1973a) studied the order of acquisition of transitivity, conservation and class inclusion in six and seven-year-olds. He found the sequence to be transitivity followed by conservation followed by classification. This is inconsistent with Piaget's sequence. Brainerd recognised that this discrepancy could be due to a failure to equate (and hence properly compare) methodologies. We will argue later that this is not a convincing defence if one is to be consistent within Piaget's general structural theory. Quite simply, the structures Piaget describes as underlying intellectual performance should, in his terms, be resistant to the specific demands of a task in a particular class. The problems posed by discrepancies evidently arising from specific task demands are discussed more extensively in the section on horizontal décalage. Suffice to say at this point that persistently occurring 'methodological problems' may have at their root, fundamental conceptual problems.

Another issue in this section on the universality of sequence, is the question, 'Does the theory predict that everyone will attain all the stages?' It is frequently found that formal operational thinking is absent in primitive societies (see Dasen, 1972, for a review). Indeed formal operational thinking is by no means universal amongst highly educated Western students (Wason and Johnson-Laird, 1972). Equally, in many non-technological societies only about 50 per cent of adults perform successfully on the conservation tests of the concrete operational stage (Greenfield, 1966; Dasen, 1972). Additionally, it has been shown that 61 per cent of a sample of female university students enrolled in the first year of a mathematical course did not conserve volume (Towler and Wheatley, 1971) and 18 per cent of 138 postgraduate students tested by Rowell and Renner (1976) failed tests of conservation of volume.

The absence of formal operational thinking in certain societies or the majority of adults in any society is no problem to the theory as such. Piaget (1972a) acknowledged that a great number of normal adults might never reach the stage of formal operations and those who did might do so only in areas of specific interest to them. Additionally, Piaget noted that, 'the growth of formal thinking . . . remains dependent on social as much as and more than on neurological factors' and that, 'A particular social environment remains indispensable for the realisation of these possibilities' (Inhelder and Piaget, 1958, p. 337).

Lacunae in concrete operational thinking in large sections of populations or in significant percentages of highly educated adults are not so easily discounted. In Piaget's theory conservation is a necessary condition for all rational thought (Piaget and Szeminska, 1952). It must be said that since the theory does not predict that all humans will reach the stage of concrete operations the finding that great numbers of them do not and that others have curious gaps in their concrete operational thinking is no direct challenge to the theory. However, given the status assigned to these attainments, these findings are very odd. This is particularly so since the people who fail in these respects are no less able at performing in their societies than those who pass. For example, Heron (1971) showed that the attainment of weight conservation in Zambian children bore no relationship to measures of ability and scholastic achievement and similarly Schwebel (1975) showed that logical thinking assessed in terms of Piagetian formal operations had almost no relationship to high school rank in mathematics tests. Schwebel noted that,

> Two subjects with approximately equivalent high school rank . . . perform as differently as this: Given a balance scale and freedom to experiment with it at will, one will be unable even to achieve balance by use of unequal weights, while the other, after experimenting, will propose a general rule enabling him to predict equilibrium under varying circumstances (M. Schwebel (1975), pp. 139–40).

Clearly, whilst such data do not sink the theory (or even damage it) they do raise questions about the significance of Piagetian tasks and the acquisitions they are said to mark. This question of significance is discussed later.

The final question to be appraised in the examination of the ubiquity of stages and stage sequence, is the question of developmental lag. Some societies are found to be several years behind Westerners in the acquisition of, for example, conservation. What is to be made of this? The theory makes no claim about a ubiquitous *rate* of development. At no stage in theoretical discussion is age considered as an important variable. Usually ages are given in data only to communicate sequence or to give some sense of order in development. Thus findings of developmental lag, however large, are entirely expected and do not challenge the theory. Indeed,

> One finds in children of the same town, depending on the individuals, and on the social, family or school environments, advances or delays that are often considerable. These do not contradict the order of succession, which remains constant, but show that other factors are added to the epigenetic mechanisms (J. Piaget, 1976, p. 261).

It is fair to say however, that in so easily.dismissing these lags or accelerations, opportunities are lost to explore which factors influence development and in what manner they operate. Indeed one might reasonably expect that a theory of development should say something more specifically about the role of experience.

In this section we have looked at three aspects of the claim of universal sequence. First, we have shown that on the clear and fundamental claim to universal sequence there are studies which run counter to the prediction and others which, whilst at a general or average level supporting the sequence, contain individuals who do not. Second, we have shown that for many people the top end of the hierarchy is missing or limited in scope, and third that there is a wide range of rates at which the developmental sequence is attained. These last two pose no *direct* challenge to any prediction the theory makes and indeed conform to theoretical expectations. However, in so far as no clear account of these phenomena is provided and since truncated development or slow development does not seem to disadvantage people in comparison with their peers it is legitimate to expect the theory to handle rather than dismiss such findings. This is discussed further in the section on the role of experience in cognitive development.

Is there a coherent universal structure amongst operations in a given stage?

Imagine two children, one born and raised in London and the other born and socialised in the Australian outback. Suppose, also, that they are both in the stage of concrete operations.

It is Piaget's contention that whilst mental contents might differ radically, the processes which they apply in thinking do not. Mental contents differ, mental processes in a given stage do not. It is fundamental to the theory that a stage is defined by a coherent, organised corpus of operations or mental processes. If a child is able to deduce that *A* is bigger than *C* having been told that *A* is bigger than *B* and *B* is bigger than *C* then he should be able to do the problem whether the *A*, *B* and *C* refer to heights of children, heights of walls or heights of trees. The particular content, according to Piaget's theory, does not matter if the child is in possession of the underlying intellectual processes necessary to the task. If a child is in the stage of concrete operations he should be able to demonstrate this status consistently on tasks judged to demand concrete operations.

Contrary to the theory however, a great deal of evidence suggests that content matters very much indeed. For example Cole (1975) gave the problem shown in Figure 3.1 to members of the Kpelle tribe of Liberia.

The subject is taught that pushing a button in box *A* will

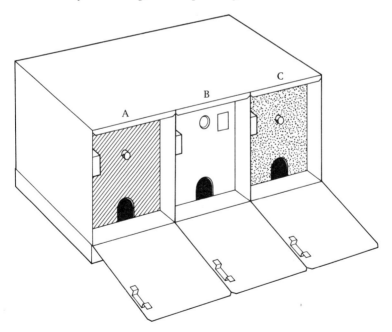

Figure 3.1. *Cole's apparatus (from M. Cole, 1975, p. 167)*

yield a marble whilst pushing a button in box C yields a ball bearing. He is also taught that putting the ball bearing in box B yields a piece of candy. This is a problem widely used to assess inferential ability in American children. The child has to relate the 'premises' (how to get a ball bearing and how to use a ball bearing) to the solution (how to get candy). Kpelle performance on this task was very poor. Only 15 per cent of young adults solved the problem spontaneously. However, when an analogous problem was made up out of matchboxes and a small locked chest even Kpelle children performed proficiently. This might be taken to imply that 'familiarity with the materials about which one is asked to reason is important if people are going to apply a cognitive skill they have' (M. Cole, 1975, p. 168).

The possession of the underlying capacity to make these kinds of inferences is *necessary* to solve this kind of problem, but it is by no means sufficient. Familiarity with the materials is helpful, if not crucial, in evoking the pertinent intellectual processes.

There are many studies of non-Western cultures which show that performance on conservation tasks is dependent on the material used in the tests (Cole, Gray, Glick and Sharp, 1971, Goodnow, 1969b). On searching for patterns of performance across a number of tests given in a variety of cultures, Goodnow was forced to conclude that, 'one would become cautious about assuming "conservation" to be a skill more general than it is content specific' (J. Goodnow, 1969b, p. 250).

Clearly, on presenting a child with a task, whether a particular mental operation will be revealed or not depends quite critically on the particular task used. When the same competences are claimed to define performance across a number of tasks and this claim is put to the test, an even greater degree of heterogeneity of performance is revealed. We have already described the model of concrete operational thinking said to account for intellectual performance at that stage. At the heart of the stage notion there is claimed to be a unity of operations. Thus children competent at several concrete operational tasks should be expected to be competent at most other concrete operational tasks. In the light of the above studies it will come as no surprise that this is not the case. In a study of Papuan children (Heron and Dowel, 1978) aged ten to sixteen years, non-verbal tests of conservation of weight and a wide-ranging set of tests of reasoning were given. There were three main sets of reasoning tasks which involved completing matrices which required the child to make perceptual judgments, judgments based on counting or judgments based on making multi-dimensional comparisons. Of the 109 children tested about half were conservers. It was found that in general the non-conservers showed evidence of reasoning ability almost equivalent to that of the conservers. Five of the non-conservers solved every one of the eighteen reasoning tasks presented. In another study (Heron and Dowel, 1973) the capacity of non-conservers of weight to achieve operational solutions of multiple classification tasks was investigated. Forty-nine Yugoslav immigrants to Australia were tested. Their average age was ten years and all had been in Australia for between twelve and twenty-four months. It was found that one third of the non-conservers of weight gave operational solutions to seven out of eight multiple classification tasks. Given these data it is difficult to conceive of the concrete operational stage as a formal unity (Heron and Dowel, 1973, p. 8).

Thus cross-cultural studies have confirmed what studies more locally conceived have found. First, there seems to be little about performance on tasks ostensibly tapping the same operations which would allow us to conclude that these operations could be used to account for task performance. In other words, there is so much variability in performance which is unpredictable from the point of view of Piaget's operational model. Second, postulated relations between operations, i.e. the *structures d'ensemble* which define stage performance, are not able either to predict the data obtained nor give any account of its heterogeneity when a range of tasks tapping these structures is given to groups of children within a stage.

This lack of relationship between performances amongst stage-related tasks, or conversely, the task specificity of performance, creates extensive problems of interpretation. How many concrete operational tasks should a child fail before we decide he is not in the stage of concrete operations? Were the conclusions regarding truncated development reported in the previous section based on unfamiliar tasks? Would non-technological societies show developmentally more mature levels of thought if we used Cole's technique to look for processes? That is, should we find task analogues which retain the need for particular mental operations whilst allowing us to alter the materials to those more familiar to the subjects? If we keep tasks constant across a range of cultures we are prone to assign differences in performance to differences in culture. If we use a range of tasks within a culture we are likely to assign differences in performance to differences in tasks.

The problem must not be seen as merely methodological. At the heart of this issue is the problem of diagnosing mental contents. There are underlying conceptual problems here. How is a particular competence to be conceived? How may particular performances be interpreted? How is performance related to underlying competence? This excursion into cross-cultural studies has brought these problems into sharp relief. The competence-performance distinction was raised in Chapter 2 and is discussed briefly at the end of this chapter and more extensively in Chapter 4.

In the light of these difficulties the existence of coherent, universal structures amongst operations seems questionable.

Are there different routes to intellectual acquisitions?

Do differences in environmental stimulation affect only the rate of intellectual development or do they also influence the *course* of this development? Are intellectual acquisitions (such as the conservations) constructed by similar intellectual processes? It is easy to assume for example, that the conservation of continuous quantity exhibited by Aborigines and that exhibited by the Londoner, whilst arising out of different particular experiences, still rest on the development of identical intellectual processing. The Piagetians put the question thus,

> Does the development of the fundamental mental operations follow one particular pattern, regardless of the type and amount of schooling a child may receive, or, on the contrary, are there different ways of acquiring a particular type of reasoning? (Inhelder, Sinclair and Bovet, 1974, p. 118).

This is a very important question. For one thing it takes us beyond the stage description level of studying cognitive development and into the more fundamental problem of *accounting* for that development. Second, to be open to empirical investigation it demands that theorists specify the processes of development in ways sufficiently clear and unambiguous to be testable, and third it is the kind of question which guides the exploration of how we might account for the notable differences in the rate of acquisition of cognitive structures. In the light of the importance attached to this question (Inhelder, Sinclair and Bovet, 1974; Piaget, 1976) it is unfortunate that very few studies have been addressed to it. This is probably due to the lack of specification of the routes to acquisition. However, it is clear that Piagetian theory predicts a particular route to particular acquisitions—a prediction seen as open to cross-cultural examination. For example,

> But if the equilibration factors can be hypothesised to be very general and relatively independent of the social environment, this hypothesis requires cross-cultural verification. Equilibration processes can be observed in particular in the formation of the concepts of conservation, the stages of which show, in our society, not only a sequential order, but also systems of *compensations* (Piaget, 1976, p. 261) (his emphasis).

In this instance Piaget is predicting that the development and use of a set of compensations is *the* route to the acquisition of the conservations.

The Genevan view of the acquisition of conservation is that it is 'characterised by a gradual comparison of the dimensions which later results in their coordination by compensation—an indication of conservation based on a system of operations' (Inhelder, Sinclair and Bovet, 1974, p. 128). With respect to testing this hypothesis they note,

> The intrinsic characteristics of the latter are typical of regulations according to successive levels. But are these particular stages found everywhere? If so, one would not yet have a confirmation of the hypothesis, but at least a more or less favourable indication. If not, it would be, on the contrary, the sign of particular cultural and educational influences (ibid., p. 261).

Two studies which have tested this particular hypothesis

directly are examined below. Let us be clear what is at issue. The Genevan view is that there *are* particular routes to particular acquisitions and that the hypothesis is open to cross-cultural investigation. The alternative hypothesis is that different educational or societal experiences provide different routes to the same acquisitions. The acquisition studied by the experiments reported below is that of conservation of substance which the Genevans claim to be based on a system of dimensional comparison and compensation (see Chapter 2, p. 36).

Bovet (1974) used illiterate Algerian children in her studies exploring the routes to the conservation of continuous quantity. The fifty-one children between the ages of six and twelve years were each given tests in three phases. In the first phase the traditional Genevan procedure was followed. It was established that equal quantities of water were present in each of two identical jars. One of these quantities was then poured into a jar of different diameter and the standard questions were asked. In phase two—an 'experience' phase—one glass full of water was placed alongside several others of different diameters. Each child was asked to predict the height the water would reach in each of these jars if it were poured from the full jar. Pouring was then carried out and the child could see how right or wrong he had been. Six predictions were required in all. Additionally, in this phase, each child was asked to pour equal quantities into glasses of different diameters.

In the third phase of the study the tests of phase I were repeated in order to assess the impact of phase II on levels of conservation. The results are illustrated in the following table.

	Age (years)			
	6–7	7–8	8–9	9–10
Phase				
I Traditional conservation tests	NC	C ——$\overset{1}{\longrightarrow}$ Int		C
II Experience phase		$\Big\downarrow$ 2		
III Conservation tests repeated	NC	NC Int	Int	C

Two curious changes are marked by the arrows. In the pre-test the children of eight to nine performed at a less mature

standard than the children of seven to eight. This runs counter to all Genevan expectations. The second arrow marks an
apparent regression for the seven- to eight-year-olds consequent upon the experience phase. This group of Algerian
seven- to eight-year-olds certainly appears unusual in terms of
Genevan theory. Bovet notes that in phase I of the study
they unhesitatingly gave conservation type answers but
would not give any justifications. In phase II they were quite
inconsistent in answers to prediction problems and did not
seem to learn from their errors.

What is to be made of such observations? Bovet admits,

> The Algerian experiments . . . thus seem to point to dif-
> ferent developmental patterns . . . such differences in the
> development of . . . concepts are of far more interest for
> cross-cultural research than variations in the ages at which
> children in different populations acquire certain concepts
> (Inhelder, Sinclair and Bovet, 1974, p. 125).

However, in assessing the *significance* of these interesting
differences she is dismissive for the following reasons:

1 they are temporary differences;
2 the 'rogue' conservation responses of the 7–8-year-olds
   are given without justification and
3 the training session brings the children back on the
   Genevan track.

That is, after training the seven- to eight-year-olds begin to
make dimensional contrasts. Regrettably there are more
problems in interpreting this study than Bovet chooses to
mention. First the study is cross-sectional in design, thus the
'natural' regression from seven to eight years to eight to nine
years refers to two different groups of children and to claim
that the training experience brings the seven- to eight-year-
olds back on the Genevan track does not show that this
would be the track they would naturally follow in their
development. Additionally, no data are given about the time
lapse between phase I and phase II testing and neither were
any tests given it appears, after phase III to explore the
longer term effects of phase II experiences. Without these
data, usually considered essential to training studies, we cannot discriminate between maturation and training effects, nor
establish whether training had had its effects at an operational
level or merely at a responding level. We suggest that Bovet

too readily dismisses her unusual phase I findings. If the finding is left as it stands it does not, of course, demonstrate that these Algerian children take different routes to conservation; in showing that they do not follow the Piagetian hierarchy however, the need for further investigation of this possibility is evident.

In an earlier study of the development of the conservation of continuous quantity (Greenfield, 1966) African children were compared with US children on standard Genevan tests and on various training procedures. Greenfield studied Wolof children living in Senegal. She used three age groups, six to seven years, eight to nine years and eleven to thirteen years. Each age group of Africans was made up of children living in various degrees of urbanisation, rural unschooled, rural schooled and urban schooled. The tests used throughout were the traditional Genevan tests of conservation of continuous quantity using water. Initial equivalence was agreed and then one quantity was poured into jars of various diameters. Greenfield's results were taken to support her conviction that 'differently encultured children have basically different schemata for approaching conservation' (Greenfield, 1969, p. 237).

In contrasting the performance of the Wolof children with US children examined in a previous study Greenfield notes that there was a very similar pattern of reasons given *in favour* of conservation but in justifying their *non-conservation* responses the Wolofs used direct action reasons to explain perceptual discrepancies in 20 per cent of cases. Thus they would comment, 'There is more in this glass because you poured it' for example. This type of reasoning has been termed 'action magic'. 'It is that form of "magical thinking" in which natural phenomena are explained by attributing special powers to intervening human agents' (Greenfield, 1969, p. 227).

It was Greenfield's contention that these children are seduced less by perception than by the experimenter's actions. To explore this view she studied the effect of two forms of training. In one case the act of pouring was carried out behind a screen and the children were asked to make their judgments prior to seeing the effects of pouring. This effect of screening is known to produce more mature conservation responses in US non-conservers. It has little effect on the Wolofs as can be seen in the following table.

Effect of screening

Post-screening responses of a group of US and Wolof non-conserving children

	US %	Wolof %
non-conserver	27	87
fluctuator	37	10
conserver	36	3

This effect is entirely consistent with Greenfield's view that screening helps the US child to avoid perceptual confusions but does not help the Wolof to avoid the effects of action magic. In the next training study, Greenfield examined the effect of allowing the Wolof children to do the pouring themselves. For a variety of reasons the number of children involved in this particular phase of the study was small but the results were quite dramatic. In a group of six- to seven-year-olds only 25 per cent of those who observed adults pouring gave conservation responses whilst 67 per cent of those who did their own pouring gave conservation responses. For a group aged eight to ten years the proportions giving conservation responses were less than a half of 'observers' but 82 per cent of 'actives'. Perhaps most importantly action magic reasons disappeared altogether when the child did the pouring whereas when the adult poured, such justifications made up 25 per cent of all reasons. The action magic reasons were replaced by identity reasons (i.e. references to the original state of the system). It is the differential effects of these instructional methods (i.e. the training procedures) together with a comparison of the different reasons given for responses by pre-conservers that led Greenfield to conclude that whilst the essence of conservation is universal 'the techniques by which it can be implanted are not' (Greenfield, 1969, p. 240), and that,

If these experiments indicate one thing of special importance, it is the way in which different modes of thought can lead to the same results. . . . We have shown how an identity schema is as crucial to conservation in Senegal as in the United States, but that it can develop by different means (ibid., pp. 244, 245).

This apparent demonstration of different routes to the same end is not accepted by Genevan critics. It is noted by Bovet (1974) for example, that the screening and pouring procedures used by Greenfield simply direct the children to the particular aspect of the situation, 'which elicits correct *answers* to the conservation question, it is doubtful however, whether these responses indicate a better *understanding* of the problem' (Bovet, op. cit., 1974, p. 129).

It will be recalled that we made exactly the same criticisms of her study. Cross-sectional investigations of this problem or training studies without longer term testing will always be open to this kind of comment. What Bovet cannot dismiss however is that, in Greenfield's study, different interventions had different effects with different children and in exactly the manner predicted. We do not wish to claim, on this basis, that the debate is resolved in Greenfield's favour. Perhaps the more important contrast here is the manner in which the cross-cultural problem is conceived and tackled by these two workers. Both studies are genuinely cross-cultural; Bovet contrasts Algerian children with Swiss children, Greenfield compares Wolofs with US children. Both carried out all the testing in the child's native language. Both supplemented a cross-sectional exploration of developmental trend with an examination of the impact of training studies. Both used only immediate post tests to examine the effects of training (and are therefore open to the criticism of not exploring 'understanding'). The crucial difference seems to us to be that Greenfield's training studies were designed to explore clearly articulated hypotheses given to account for the discrepancies observed. The training studies could have given results consistent with the hypotheses (as was the case) or could have negated these explanations. The Genevan training study on the other hand was directed at no particular account of explanation of the 'important' discrepancy found in the Algerian development. Since the seven- to eight-year-old group gave no justification for their unhesitating but precocious conservation judgments, it is difficult to imagine what account one could offer which might be testable. Indeed an absence of suitable justifications for conservation responses is generally taken, in Genevan terms, to preclude describing the child as a conserver at all. This absence of a clear, testable hypothesis in Bovet's study thus becomes justifiable in the sense that the specific problem raised by her study is not clear and hence not open to testable accounts. This is not to say that the study can be dismissed even though Bovet dismisses it herself. Rather it demonstrates an intriguing phenomenon—as does so much Genevan work—worthy of more systematic study.

For the moment, rather than concluding, on the basis of Greenfield's study alone, that there *are* different routes to similar intellectual acquisitions, we would suggest that we have commented on the problem of approaching such a question and the importance of its resolution. We end this section by making the suggestion that more progress would be made here if differences and discrepancies rather than similarities and trends were studied, and studied with clearly articulated, testable hypotheses guiding further investigations.

Cross-cultural studies of the effect of experience on cognitive development

A very large number of studies have explored the effect of experience on cognitive development (see Modgil and Modgil, 1976 for an extensive bibliography). These studies show that experience does influence cognitive growth. This less than earth-shattering conclusion has little to say about the theory and the theory has less to say about the studies. The studies themselves are rarely aimed at testing any aspect of the theory related to the role of experience and the notion of 'experience' is only very vaguely conceptualised both in these studies and in the theory.

It will be recalled that Piaget's theory adopts an inter-actionist view of cognitive development. That is, it predicts that experience, generally and specifically, influences the acquisition of cognitive structures. At the most non-specific level, 'This general coordination of actions presupposes multiple systems of autoregulation or equilibration which depend upon the environmental circumstances as well as on epigenetic potentialities' (Piaget, 1976, p. 261), and with respect to specific stages, 'the growth of formal thinking remain(s) dependent on social as much as and more than on neurological factors' (B. Inhelder and J. Piaget, 1958, p. 337).

Whilst, with reference to particular experiences, 'The child who is familiar with folding and unfolding paper shapes through his work at school is two or three years in advance of children who lack this experience' (J. Piaget and B. Inhelder, 1967, p. 276).

The two major ways in which the role of experience has been explored are (a) cross-cultural studies and (b) training studies. For the moment we shall focus on the former.

Three categories of cross-cultural study can be formed. There are those which have studied the effect of familiarity with the testing materials, those which have studied the effect of schooling and those which have examined the effect of contact with technological society. Each kind of study poses complex practical and conceptual problems. These are well illustrated by those studies attempting to determine the effect of 'familiarity' with testing materials.

It is not always easy to know whether children are familiar with the tasks, materials or related experiences. Price-Williams (1961) for example, studied the conservation of continuous and discontinuous quantity amongst West African Bush children. He noted that because these children had no formal instruction in number their levels of acquisition gave some support to a neurophysiological account of conservation attainment. Since then, Okonji (1971) and Furby (1971) have noted that these children belong to a tribe in which a game very similar to the conservation tasks is played. This is clearly less than 'formal instruction'; how far does it count as familiarity?

Familiarity is not an all or nothing experience and 'degree of familiarity' is a very difficult dimension to conceptualise. Deregowski and Serpell (1971) for example, examined classification behaviours in Zambian and Scots children. The two groups did not differ significantly when the stimulus materials to be sorted were toys but the Zambians performed at lower levels than the Scots when photographs of toys became the stimuli; i.e. degree of familiarity (toys over photographs of toys) was taken to have influenced levels of classification. But there are more differences between toys and photographs of toys than mere familiarity and those differences allow a range of new variables to be used as a basis of classification. What photographs have in common (e.g. they are generally all two dimensional, same size, same perspective, black and white) is impressive and could afford a basis for classification quite apart from the subject matter of the photographs. The familiarity/unfamiliarity dimension is unlikely to be a unitary dimension even when so concretely exemplified as in this study.

In a commonsense way we talk of being 'more or less familiar' with some material or experience. We are all more or less familiar with the workings of a motor car for example. How this degree of familiarity helps us on a particular task depends very much on the task. For some tasks familiarity rapidly reaches a ceiling level.

One needs to know little enough about the workings of a car to recognise one on sight. However, greater degrees of familiarity are necessary if one wants to put petrol in a car or to change the oil or change the clutch plate. The point here is that, in ignorance of both task and degree of familiarity it is difficult to conceptualise the interactive relationships between familiarity of material and task performance in such a way as to produce testable hypotheses. The bland 'familiarity is related to performance' is a truism. Large numbers of studies have taken great trouble to underwrite this claim with empirical data. For example Za'rour (1971) tested 132 Lebanese children on conservation of weight problems. The children were between seven and nine years, eight months and the materials used were plasticine, rubber bands and alcohol in thermometers. Conservation performance with plasticine was equivalent to US children of the same age but performance with rubber bands and the alcohol in thermometers was inferior. Experience *is* in some way related to performance. But in what way and by what means? *Ad hoc* explanations are rampant.

Price-Williams *et al.* (1969) showed that children of potters conserved quantity earlier than children of non-pottery making families, evidently 'because of experience' but Greenfield (1974) showed that flower sellers of the Zinacanticos of Southern Mexico grouped familiar objects (flowers) by colours more poorly than non-familiar objects apparently 'because of the irrelevance of the colour dimension to flower bouquets in the context of Zinacantico culture' (Greenfield, 1974, p. 158). Clearly data and explanation of this sort have little to say about any theory. Such data are consistent with Piaget's view of the role of experience. Equally they are consistent with other theories of cognitive development, including, for example, Bruner's, or the Behaviourists and the Russian theories outlined earlier. Little progress is likely to be made either in accumulating a coherent body of findings or in a theoretical understanding of these findings and their relevance for development in general unless the concepts of familiarity and experience are more clearly specified and a theory developed which makes more specific, testable challenges to empirical work.

Those studies which have explored the effect of 'schooling' may be subjected to the same type of criticism. To show that 'schooling' has an effect on cognition is to present a finding that is consistent with all contemporary theories of cognitive development. It says little which can be taken to test predictions derived from the theory of Piaget, nor does the theory make sufficiently clear claims to direct the research which could make such constructive tests.

Problems of validating Piaget's theory by reference to cross-cultural studies

In the preceding sections we have raised more questions than we have answered. This in itself is a matter of some significance and in this section we review both the answered and unanswered questions in an attempt to draw some general conclusions regarding the theory.

Any empirical undertaking is bound to meet methodological problems. There are difficulties with measurement and performance variability, differential familiarity with tasks and problems of designing appropriate control groups so that the effects of independent variables can be assessed. Cross-cultural studies have these problems and more.

> Cross-cultural studies are only beginning, and it would be very unwise to draw conclusions, given . . . the great difficulties, linguistic and others, which there are in multiplying these studies. An additional difficulty is the long training necessary to master the testing methods, which become more difficult to use as they get closer to operational functions (J. Piaget, 1976).

The language problem may be particularly acute. In studying people of the Tiv in Central Nigeria, Price-Williams noted, 'it has to be admitted that a thorough mastery of the language was not sufficient to allow follow-up questions of the type which Piaget asks, other than the question "why?" ' (D. R. Price-Williams, 1969, p. 203). And Greenfield found that,

A major linguistic difficulty that had to be overcome was the inherent ambiguity in the Wolof language surrounding the two words for equal (*tolo* and *yem*). Both have the double sense of equal level and equal amount. Since the correct solution of the conservation problem depends on recognizing the distinction between these two 'equalities', the cognitive implications of this linguistic difficulty are substantial (P. M. Greenfield, 1969, p. 217).

We do not wish to suggest that this kind of problem makes cross-cultural comparison impossible or that Piaget's theory is the only theory which meets these difficulties. Any theory which makes claims to ubiquitous generality meets this sort of problem in testing such hypotheses. (For an interesting discussion of similar difficulties involved in testing Russian theories in Western societies see D. Bloor, 1977.) In any event the problems are not insurmountable. Greenfield, for example, resolved the ambiguity in Wolof usage by asking the children the following question, 'Does this glass of yours and this glass of mine have equal water; or does this glass of mine have more water; or does this glass of yours have more water?' (P. M. Greenfield, 1969, p. 217).

The point is that cross-cultural studies exaggerate a difficulty we are already familiar with. In Piagetian tasks experimenters' instructions and children's verbal responses are wide open to linguistic misinterpretation (Goodnow, 1973).

Equally, the implicit contextual cues presented in any experimental setting are known to have a potent influence on responses. Behaviour cannot be interpreted in absolute terms but only with reference to the context in which it takes place. In studies of cognitive development the experimenter is pre-occupied with identifying underlying cognitive processes and in consequence makes no comment on contextual influences on children's responses. A good illustration of the potency of such influences is provided by Rose and Blank (1974). They criticise the standard conservation task procedures for asking the identical question twice which they suggest would ordinarily be taken as an invitation to revise an initial response. They tested this view by carrying out conservation of discrete quantity tests with six-year-old children who were presented with the tasks in one of three conditions. One group was given the standard test in which a judgment of equality was requested, a rearrangement carried out and then a second judgment requested. The second group was asked for one judgment only and this was asked for after they had seen a rearrangement. The third group was simply asked for one judgment but without seeing a rearrangement. There was a significant superiority of judgment from the middle group— a result taken to give strong support to the hypothesis that when a child declares that his rows are equal (or unequal) he interprets a request for a second judgment as a signal to change his response. The effect of contextual cues was generalised to subsequent testing. Thus children who did one-judgment tasks first made fewer errors when they met the standard testing technique one week later, whilst those who met the standard technique first made more errors on the standard and on one judgment tasks met subsequently. The authors concluded that their data supported 'the notion that the implicit contextual cues which the child first encounters play a large role in determining the response he will employ on this and all subsequent related tasks' (Rose and Blank, 1974, p. 502).

Obviously, 'fail' responses may be perfectly valid if we know the significance of the contextual cues being used by the children in the studies. This problem of making sense of the subjective interpretation of the task and its contextual significance for the testee confounds many cross-cultural studies. It makes the interpretation of the failure of so many 'primitives' on so many tasks very difficult. Recall how less than 50 per cent of Aboriginal adults succeed in the conservation of continuous quantity (Dasen, 1972). It has been asked, 'Are we to believe that aborigine adults will store water in tall thin cans in order to "have more water"; do they think they lose water when they pour it from a bucket into a barrel?' (M. Cole, 1975, p. 171).

It seems strange that people so adept at surviving in arid conditions should be so incompetent at conserving quantity when the material is water! We thus have a dual problem; we have difficulty in interpreting the failure of a testee on a test because we do not know how he has 'read' the task and we do not understand the cultural significance of attaining the cognitive process the task is intended to assess. This has been well put by Cole and Scribner (1974).

Until we have some better idea of what induces some members of traditional societies to solve conservation problems while their neighbours do not, we cannot be certain about the significance of conservation tests as a tool for understanding the relationship between culture and cognitive development (Cole and Scribner, 1974, p. 156).

Given the problems of interpreting fail responses and given that we know that testees make contextual interpretations of tasks it is clearly exceedingly difficult to use cross-cultural studies to test the general claims of Piaget's theory. The formal equivalence of treatments of different groups does not guarantee the equivalence of operations assessed since different groups may make different interpretations of the tasks. As a consequence, inferences about lack of competence are unwarranted. This is not to say that all cross-cultural data should be abandoned as useless on these grounds, nor that cross-cultural studies are necessarily opaque in the testing of Piagetian hypotheses. Dasen (1976) has the view that differences in performance genuinely reflect cultural demand. The point at issue however, is that if we interpret Piagetian studies in the standard Genevan manner we either *assume* that particular performances are correlated with particular underlying operations (and hence we cannot test the theory) or we accept that underlying operations may *manifest* themselves in a variety of ways (including the failure on some tests as a consequence of contextual reading) in which case we have the problem of interpreting results described above. Thus a crucial methodological problem of cross-cultural research is once again seen to be a general problem exaggerated. There is an induced ethnocentrism in the methodology. We are asking how well people in other societies can do our problems when we should be asking how well they can solve their own problems. Like the language problem the difficulties created here are not insurmountable. It is perfectly possible to keep altering the arrangement, materials and instructions on particular tasks, whilst keeping the underlying cognitive processes intact, until combinations are found which people can successfully respond to. An example of this technique has already been referred to (Cole, 1975) and Cole has expanded upon this method of experimental anthropology (Cole and Scribner, 1974). Additionally it has been suggested (Ashton, 1975) that the multitrait-multimethod approach to assessing personality be imported into the assessment of cognitive processes. Essentially this method involves assessing a range of processes by a range of methods and searching amongst responses for patterns and relationships. This method, elaborated by Campbell and Fiske (1959) and Cole's approach allow interpretations to be made about the circumstances in which particular processes are evoked and utilised, and hence present opportunities for a closer examination of the availability to the testee of particular competences. These methods are not much in evidence in cross-cultural studies carried out to date.

The problems of testing Piaget's claims are not merely methodological. In Chapter 1 we described the requirements of a scientific theory. To be testable a theory needs to generate clearly expressed, unambiguous predictions or descriptions and these have to be different from those generated by other, competing theories, i.e. theories claiming to give adequate accounts of the same data or phenomena. Additionally claims made by a scientific theory must be empirically testable. We are not suggesting that theories appear on the scene fully grown and developed so that every concept is precise, every prediction crystal clear and every description unambiguous. As we have already said, theories develop, grow, increase in precision and elaboration. Concepts which are initially cloudy give way to more clarified versions in a constant interchange between conceptualisation and practical work. What is essential for conceptualisation at any stage in the development of a theory is that it be testable and open to refutation and consequent refinement.

In some of the previous sections we have shown the extensive lack of conceptualisation at an empirically testable level. This, far more than methodological problems, obstructs progress in either evaluating or refining the theory. Indeed it demonstrates well that there is no sharp distinction in many cases, between a method problem and a conceptual problem. We noted the massive amount of work, for example, on the role of experience in cognitive growth and showed that the bland conclusion that experience influenced development, whilst not detracting from Piaget's theory, was entirely consistent with all other theories of development. Workers in this field have allowed themselves to operate with variables which are far too unspecific. 'Schooling' or 'experience' are terms which have neither operational, conceptual or commonsensical specificity nor any particular or necessary manifestations. With reference to the notion of experience there has been no attention to the identification or analysis of necessary versus sufficient experiences for particular acquisitions, nor to essential versus merely helpful experience, nor to the timing of the utility of particular experiences for the acquisition of particular skills. It could be said that this lack of analysis is not the fault of the theory but a deficit in all these workers attempting to use the theory. This is rather a large defence to swallow. In any event it begs the question of why so little progress has been made in sharpening the conceptualisation of the role of learning in cognitive development.

Any conception of the role of learning and experience in Piaget's theory must arise from his model of equilibration which accounts for those processes of development based on experiential input. The equilibration model has, unfortunately, never been described at an empirically testable level of specificity. The functional concepts of assimilation and accommodation have always been viewed with some concern. They were seen by Flavell (1962) as very broad generalisations containing 'only the seeds of process rules' (p. 85) for example and recent Genevan work exploring the *processes* of development (Inhelder *et al.* 1974) shows a continuing inability to specify the functioning of these processes. The problems this creates for those who attempt to test the theory are well illustrated by reference to the work of Bovet and of Greenfield which we contrasted in an earlier section. They each ask the question, are there different routes to the same cognitive acquisition? Greenfield suggests that there are and that Piaget's theory is in error in claiming otherwise. Bovet suggests that her own work supports Piaget's view. Within the equilibration model, both sets of data could be, in a *post hoc* fashion, accommodated. The model requires only that conservation be achieved by a system of compensations. At a concrete level and with reference to the conservation of quantity it may be taken that the compensations refer to dimensional compensations. At this level, Bovet and Greenfield are at variance. But at a more abstract level only the dissonance created by two conflicting propositions need be compensated and it could be said that Greenfield's Wolofs learn to compensate between the effects of 'action magic' and the effects of their own actions. Thus the equilibration model could claim that identical processes (resolution of dissonant inputs) is at the heart of the cognitive growth although different contents are processed. At that level of generality the theory becomes untestable—a point we examine in Chapter 5.

Not all the claims of the theory are so obtuse. There are clear and unequivocal claims made about the ubiquity of the stage hierarchy and the generality of the descriptions of cognitive structure said to represent intellectual operations at a given stage. With respect to the universal nature of the hierarchical stage sequence we have shown that the great majority of studies confirm the observations made in Switzerland. We reported a number of discrepant studies but the remarks we have made about interpreting cross-cultural studies in general imply that it is extremely difficult to come to any firm conclusion. It is not clear whether the postulated universal sequence needs reconceptualising or whether studies showing discrepancies can be demonstrated to be at odds on methodological grounds. From another point of view, however, this resolution of conflicting studies may be entirely irrelevant for it can be argued that the sequentiality of the stages is not an empirical issue (Ammon, 1977; Phillips and Kelly, 1975).

A minor excursion is necessary to clarify this point. We can make observations of intellectual performance for children of different ages. It will then be possible to categorise and classify these observations in various ways. Clearly, no classification is *compelled* by nature. For a particular mode of classification or ordering of our data we could observe a particular sequence in the classes. In what sense would this sequence be a 'necessary' sequence? Is the sequence a property of the data or does its 'necessity' arise out of the way we define the categories in which we place our observations? To test the latter view we do not need data. Rather, we need to analyse logically the relationships between our categories.

Any hierarchical notion must be examined for conceptual links *prior* to empirical investigation. If someone claimed to have discovered that wicketkeepers were all cricketers we would not rush out to test this by surveying wicketkeepers. (Although we acknowledge that some social scientists would and worse, others would survey all cricketers.)

The work of Gagné (1970) provides an example more germane to the acquisition of cognitive skills. Gagné describes hierarchical structures in learning. He claims that these are psychological structures. In fact the hierarchies he describes are quite clearly definitional. For example, he shows that to learn to draw and identify the intersection of two lines one must know the rules that govern the construction of lines and their intersections. Clearly this is not a psychological theory at all and experimentation is totally irrelevant to testing it.

Now what is the status of Piaget's claim of necessary sequence? When he claims that the negotiation of one stage is necessary to the development of the next, is he claiming that this is a logical necessity arising out of the definitions of processes in the two stages, or is he claiming that this is an empirically established lawfulness? Unfortunately it is not at all easy to identify Piaget's stance on this issue. We have already referred to his comments on the observations said to underpin this claim to necessary sequence (p. 64). Elsewhere however, he has suggested,

> To characterise the stages of cognitive development we therefore need to integrate two necessary conditions without introducing any contradictions. These conditions for stages are (a) that they must be defined to guarantee a constant order of succession and (b) that the definition allow for progressive construction without entailing total preformation (Piaget, 1970b, p. 710).

Condition (a) clearly implies that the 'necessary' sequence arises out of the definition of the stages and is a consequence of those definitions; this precludes empirical test. Those cross-cultural studies which claim to confirm Piaget's sequence could be said to have confirmed his definitions of stages, a task their authors could have achieved without leaving an armchair. It is not clear what condition (b) entails.

It would help to clarify the nature of the 'necessity' of this sequence if some clear, testable account of the process of invariant development were available. We. have already made our reservations about Piaget's account of development. In this context there is a further problem. Piaget suggests,

> such equilibration processes, such self regulation, also yield necessities; we might even say that their results are more necessary than those determined by heredity . . . self regulation sets a direction compatible with a construction that becomes necessary precisely in being directed (Piaget, 1971a, p. 90).

It seems here that Piaget is claiming that it is necessary to adopt a constructivist theory. But the presence of the processes and regulations at the core of this account has to be inferred from the behaviour they are used to explain. Hence, once again, the account is untestable—if our interpretation is correct.

To summarise, Piaget's claim to a hierarchical sequence of development may be a definitional claim. If this is the case, those who have gathered data on the issue have wasted their time: the claim is *so* and any discrepancies found must be attributed to method problems or performance variability. They cannot be taken seriously in appraising the claim or re-appraising its basis.

There is one final issue we wish to comment on before leaving this evaluation of cross-cultural studies. We reviewed some of the studies which have explored the generality of Piaget's description of the cognitive structures said to represent cognitive functions in a given stage. The data quite clearly show that the degree of coherence of performance the theory has led researchers to expect is not manifest in the results. There are problems in accepting this conclusion as a refutation of this aspect of the theory. The first problem is that it is not clear what degree of coherence it would be reasonable to expect nor quite how this coherence would be exemplified in performances across various tasks. Second, Piaget's descriptions of structure are descriptions of underlying competence and we need to consider the manner in which performance data can be used to test theories of competence. These problems are discussed more fully in Chapter 4.

In this section we have examined some of the problems in using cross-cultural studies to evaluate Piaget's theory. We noted that there are methodological problems including those of language, of the ethnocentricity of tasks and the interpretation of 'fail' responses. All these are problems met in more local studies. The cross-cultural context serves to exaggerate them. More seriously, we observed that some of the claims are difficult to explore because preliminary conceptualisation of the variables and processes is rarely done (cf. the effects of 'experience'). But most fundamentally it is not clear whether some of the claims are open to empirical exploration at all. Some claims, such as the necessary hierarchical sequence of stages may be taken to be no more than definitional, whilst other claims such as the necessity of constructivist processes may be taken to be fundamental assumptions of the theory.

Chapter 4

Specific issues in the validation of Piagetian theory

Testing descriptions of competence

Following Chomsky, modern studies of linguistics and language development make a distinction between performance and competence. Performance refers to the actual acts of language production or comprehension. Competence, in this sense, does not carry its common usage of 'ability to do' but rather refers to the knowledge and rules which are necessary to particular acts or performances. Linguistic competence refers to the system of rules representing a speaker/hearer's abstract knowledge of his language. A description of competence is not a psychological theory of performance in real situations. It does not represent psychological contents or operations involved in producing or interpreting sentences. It represents the grammatical knowledge that is a necessary prerequisite to performing these operations. Various factors may impede the application of this underlying competence. Since psychological data are restricted to describing acts or performances any studies of competence are indirect and must contend with these distorting factors. Since competence cannot be studied directly one is bound to ask whether it is a useful construct in accounting for performance.

Flavell and Wohlwill (1969) imported the competence/performance distinction into the realm of cognitive development. In their view a psychological theory requires two components—a competence model and an automaton (or performance) model. The competence model is a formal, logical presentation of the structure of some cognitive domain whilst the automaton model represents the psychological processes

by which information in competence gets used in real situations. Whilst a competence model says nothing about the
processes actually used nor about the personal or task features
which aid or hinder performance it is none the less, in their
view, a crucial device without which, 'the theorist could not
define the theoretical objectives of his psychological model—
he would not know what the model was to be a model of'
(1969, p. 72). Thus to describe cognitive development with
respect to some particular domain (the development of a set
of mathematical concepts for example) would require a clear
description of the knowledge and processes necessary to
operating in this domain. This description would be stated in
structural terms using concepts such as rule, plan or operation since such concepts transcend particular responses.

It is a matter of contention as to whether Piaget's theory is
a competence model or not. In 1969 it was Flavell and Wohlwill's view that it was not only a competence model, but
almost the only such model available. 'As to organisation,
Piaget's structural models (his groupings, groups and lattices)
constitute virtually the only available suggestions as to how
cognitive elements might be interrelated at each level of
development' (1969, p. 75).

It is our view that Piaget's descriptions represent accounts
of underlying competence. We can find no account of how
the contents of mental acts are selected, organised or se-
quenced or of how operating or performance characteristics
such as memory or attention limit responses. There is only
scant reference to task features which might impede performance (the 'resistance' of certain materials in conservation
studies for example). On the other hand the structures posited
are presented as quite general once acquired. In Chapter 3
we illustrated the procedural bankruptcy of treating Piaget's
account of transitive inference as if it were a performance
account.

Additionally, recent Genevan training studies have been
conceived in terms of competence. Inhelder *et al.* (1974)
noted that, 'The transitions from one state of knowledge to
the following . . . can thus be seen . . . as transformations
which account for modifications in the subject's cognitive
competence' (p. 5). Later they announced that, 'The operatory
structures studied in the learning experiments are those that
underlie the child's capacity . . .' (p. 9). On these grounds we

take Piaget's formal descriptions as a model of competence. Thus it is not a psychological theory at all. This is not to say it cannot be evaluated.

In the following sections we explore some of the problems of appraising an account of competence. In any event, such an account seen as a necessary preamble to a psychological theory, may be extrapolated to produce empirically testable predictions and we comment on evaluating a competence model by means of such studies.

Appraising a competence model

A number of complex and interrelated methodological and theoretical issues are raised in such an endeavour. Many of these problems are well illustrated by reference to a recent study of the effect of task differences on the performance of children notionally in the stage of formal operations (Martorano, 1977). Martorano selected ten tasks from 'The Growth of Logical Thinking' (Inhelder and Piaget, 1958) which had been used to obtain performance protocols from young adolescents. The protocols were then used to illustrate the general logical properties of the formal operational schemata. These general properties are,

1 that they all show some logical relationship to the combinatorial system and the INRC group,
2 that they are general processes applicable to many content areas and
3 that they are derived from the underlying cognitive structure rather than from objects in the environment (Martorano, 1977) i.e. the schemata are formal descriptions of underlying competence.

How does this competence manifest itself? Martorano used 80 children ranging in age from eleven years seven months to seventeen years, five months. All tests were given individually and all scoring used the schedules described by Piaget and Inhelder. She found that 33 per cent of subjects varied by two sub-stages in their performances across tasks and 61 per cent varied by three sub-stages. She concluded that, 'a formal operational level of performance on one task does not imply an equivalent level of performance on all tasks' (1977, p. 671).

But does the child 'possess' or not 'possess' formal operational competence? The tasks vary widely in structure and content. The number of variables across tasks varies. Questions asked of the child, even when presented in standard form, refer to specific contents and procedures and cannot, therefore, be directly compared. Descriptions of protocols show similar specific effects and scoring procedures are difficult to compare across tasks. Thus the tasks do not only make different demands on the subject of the experiment, they make different demands on the experimenter in interpreting and evaluating performance. We have to ask, how adequate (i.e. complete and general) is the description of structure which the experimenter has available and how does the underlying competence described manifest itself in behaviour? These two issues, the soundness of the description and the criterion problem, are discussed below.

Piaget's description of competence

In Chapter 2 we set out Piaget's stage descriptions in some detail. How far are these descriptions adequate? We can judge this in part by asking how far Piaget's use of symbolic logic is sensible or conventional or meaningful to contemporary scholars. Alternatively we can ask whether his model contains all that is necessary and sufficient to account for the data describing performances at a given stage. We shall now attempt to clarify the 'competence' issue by examining these areas.

Piaget's logic and conventional logicians

Logicians have expressed some perplexity at the way in which Piaget employs symbolic logic to exemplify the structure of groupings and groups (Ennis, 1975; Parsons, 1960). Their arguments are complex, and demand a knowledge of symbolic logic which we will not assume. None the less, some of their important criticisms are worthy of note.

In Chapter 2 (p. 38) we employed the symbols p and q to represent Gas C and substance B respectively. These may be combined together into what Piaget calls elements; $p.q$, 'p and q', $(\bar{p}.q)$ 'not p but q', etc. The absence of an element is taken to indicate that that combination was not observed.

But in symbolic logic this is not how the elements are used. The symbols p and q are conventionally used as *propositions* which simply have 'true' or 'false' values; and an element may not be excluded but must be examined and found necessarily false; i.e. $(p.q)$ 'if p then q' is true or false.

Piaget's system (Inhelder and Piaget, 1958) extends the convention of p and q to include *propositional functions*, that is, specific instances rather than general propositions. Conventionally the combination of propositions should be expressed as:

$$(p.q) \ V \ (\bar{p}.q) \ V \ (p.\bar{q}) \ V \ (\bar{p}.\bar{q})$$

wherein one or more of the propositions is true, the remainder false, but not absent.

The confusion of proposition with particularised propositional function, and of untruth with absence, leads to complexity. Ennis (1975) offers the following exemplification:

> If anyone grabs these two wires, that person will be shocked. . . . I know that generalisation to be true of two wires in my house, but there is no case of 'p.q', that is, of a person who has grabbed the two wires and was shocked. . . . According to the given (existence, not possibility) interpretation of Piaget's combination, the lack of such a case shows that the implication is mistaken (p. 17).

The difference is crucial, for if Piaget is suggesting that the *structure* of operations is the structure of propositional logic, he is referring to a system which is based upon the truth or falsity of elements, whether discovered or undiscovered. On the other hand, if he is using a totally idiosyncratic form of propositional logic (as Ennis and Parsons suggest) he is using an empirical form of logic. The latter is not simply a sub-set of the propositional logic, but can, in fact lead to quite different conclusions.

Ennis again offers a clear example: if we consider two propositional functions. *If* x *is a United States President, then* x *is a male*. This would be true because:

1 There is a case of a president who is male $(p.q)$
2 There is a case of a non-president who is male $(\bar{p}.q)$
3 There is a case of a non-president who is not male $(\bar{p}.\bar{q})$
4 There is no case of a president who is not male: i.e. $(p.\bar{q})$ excluded

By exclusion of (4) we obtain $(p.q) \ V \ (\bar{p}.q) \ V \ (\bar{p}.\bar{q})$ which is deemed sufficient to confirm the proposition. Yet in terms of *potential* this is clearly an over-generalisation. As an element consisting of true/false propositions *p.q* can obviously exist. Only by considering the set of *observed* events can it be discounted. Piaget is therefore implying that the logical structure derived from action presupposes an isomorphism between *observed* and *possible* events; but the formula for implication is supposed to generate an inductive judgment. His conclusion is dependent upon induction.

Piaget's commitment to structuralism leads him to seek a complete, integrated and closed system as the basis for an operational stage. Of the sixteen binary operations (Chapter 2, p. 39) which are possible, the only complete derivation is asserted by Bynum, Thomas and Weitz (1972) to be that from the task entitled 'The Role of Invisible Magnetism' (Inhelder and Piaget, 1958). Their attempts to replicate the analysis led them to conclude that the original was faulty, and that only eight of the operations could be found. Furthermore they stated that they have never found examples of certain of the operations specified either in texts or in attempts to replicate Piaget's work. In particular they reported the absence of non-implication, converse implication, complete negation and complete affirmation.

Further points have been made by Isaacs (1951). He noted that the grouping calculus is restricted in its operation to the bivalent logic of states which are 'true' or 'not true'. This excludes the vast majority of human judgments which operate on states of probability and uncertainty. Most quantities handled in everyday reasoning are of the 'more or less' sort. A more subtle extension of the same point is that in common usage even logically unambiguous notions such as 'and' or 'not' or 'true' or 'false' are not at all unambiguous. Isaacs was not suggesting that formal theories should use ambiguous terms but that they should be capable of grappling with the fact that human interpretation of the terms in everyday situations is by no means unequivocal.

The above criticisms are very general and suggest that serious limitations are written into Piaget's system. Other critics have had more specific reservations about particular aspects of the theory. Martin (1976), for example, closely analysed some of the topological tasks used by Piaget in his exploration of the child's concept of space (Piaget and Inhelder, 1967). Martin argues that Piaget uses key mathematical

terms in an imprecise way and tha͘   ͻn his loose terminology, some of the tasks useᵈ   ͻe about topology
at all. For example, it is noͺ   Piaget uses the term
'proximity' in two ways
  1 to describe the relationship of 'nearbyness' and
  2 to label a set of points or a region that has this 'nearby-
     ness' relationship with a given point or with a given ob-
     ject.
Martin suggests that in these senses the notion of proximity
is not a topological property (p. 17) and argues that, 'this is
not to say that proximity, even if all that is meant by the
term is some crude notion of closeness, is unworthy of study
nor that it is unrelated to the development of mathematical
concepts. However, if the representational space is proposed
to be topological on the basis of proximity, it would appear
axiomatic that proximity be a topological property' (Martin,
1976, p. 20). This kind of comment casts doubt on Piaget's
claim that topological representation precedes Euclidean
representation because it becomes a moot point whether
Piaget has researched in topological representation.
  In a similar vein Piaget's use of the logic of classes to give
an account of number development has been criticised (Mac-
Namara, 1975). Piaget (1952) has argued that the development of an understanding of number grows from an understanding of the logic of classes and the development of
seriation as a procedure for distinguishing between members
of a class. Macnamara points out several flaws in this view.
First, children actually master number before they master the
logic of classes. Second, class operations are different from
arithmetic operations. Third, classes are groups made of objects because they share certain attributes, whereas arithmetic
procedures can be applied (and *are* applied by young children)
to sets of objects, i.e. to arbitrary collections of objects.
Finally, seriation cannot be used to distinguish between
members of a class because one must be able to so distinguish
as a pre-requisite to seriation. With these points in mind it
would appear that Piaget's view of the development of number comprehension as an offshoot of the development of
logic is untenable.
  We have set out some criticisms of Piaget's use of symbolic
logic as a structural account of competence. We have recorded
instances of idiosyncratic and perplexing forms, of loose

usage of technical terms, of limitations built into the system's capacity to handle probabilistic propositions and of uncritical extrapolation of logical forms to account for the development of arithmetic processes. In many respects the description seems inaccurate and inadequate.

We turn now from an analysis of the logic of the system to an assessment of the model of competence by means of the empirical study of performance.

Structuralism as a conceptual framework

There is nothing implicit in the study of cognitive development which necessitates that, at any particular time, an individual's various cognitive acts will be characteristic of some unified, underlying structure. Indeed a theorist with environmentalist inclinations might be very hard pressed to justify such a notion. For him, the cognitive behaviour manifest within a given context would be dependent upon previous experiences of that context, and there would be no reason to expect it to share a common structure with behaviours elicited in other contexts. Piaget's theory, however, rests heavily upon a structuralist view, although as we observed in Chapter 3 it is by no means clear whether the view is empirically derived or whether it is a logical necessity of his means of analysis.

Piaget (1971a) describes structuralism as,

first, an ideal (perhaps a hope) of intrinsic intelligibility supported by the postulate that structures are self-sufficient . . . ; second, certain insights—to the extent that one has succeeded in actually making out certain structures, their theoretical employment has shown that structures in general have, despite their diversity, certain common and perhaps necessary properties (p. 45).

A structure is seen as something much more than a collection of elements. It is a self-contained system comprising three ideas: *wholeness, transformation,* and *self-regulation.*

The idea of wholeness is perhaps the most obvious feature of a structure. Wholeness differentiates a structure from an aggregate of elements by insisting that the elements themselves are subordinate to the *laws* which relate them. Thus, in the stage of concrete operations the individual judgments of transitivity, class inclusion, reversibility, etc., whilst disparate at the level of mere surface description, are seen to belong to an operational structure when analysed in terms of the formal logic of groupings.

If it is the laws of relationship which comprise the whole-ness of a structure, then they too must be related one to another. The transformations which relate the laws of a structure are transformations of a closed system. That is, they can provide the interplay between laws or between ele-ments, as seen in the relationship between the multiplication rule and the division rule where one is the reciprocal of the other; but they 'never yield results external to the system' (1971a, p. 5). To this extent Piaget's choice of propositional logic to analyse concrete operations *could not admit* of ele-ments outside his structures. In other words, a concrete operation could not, by definition, yield transformational products of pre-operational or formal structures.

The third property of a structure is self-regulation. In its most frequent usage this term describes the action of trans-formations in regulating the structure during transformation.

All of this theorising is at a level much divorced from the observation of cognitive behaviour. Yet it is essential to our understanding of Piaget's analyses. His belief, or hope, that underlying structures unify the cognitive acts of a given stage has a crucial influence on what he observes and how he describes it. This raises once more the issue of the interaction between the nature of data themselves, and the constructions which are placed upon them by the methods of analysis. As we have already seen Piaget's language of logic is not an orthodox one, and the 'wholeness' of an operational structure may not be evident in cognitive behaviours of any individual at any particular time; the structuralist description is of competence and not performance.

Some empirical implications of a structuralist theory:
evidence of 'wholeness'

Piagetian theory maintains that throughout development there is such qualitative change in cognitive processing that it is possible to describe stages. Basically a stage is a coherent integration of operations into a theme, or a series of themes, which underlie all, or most, cognitive acts at that point in time. This orchestration of themes is a *structure d'ensemble*. We have already examined the theoretical roots of this orchestration. The prediction which can be tested is that we should be able to uncover this unity empirically. Before embarking on such a venture there are some important qualifications built into the theory.

A stage does not come about by some instantaneous transformation. During a preparatory phase the defining structures lack stability, and will appear sporadically in conjunction with behaviours characteristic of the preceding stage. Stability will only gradually be achieved, at which time a fully orchestrated *structure d'ensemble* should be detectable. As the next stage becomes imminent more sophisticated behaviours will begin to appear, intermingling with the established structures. So the experimenter should be prepared to find cognitive disturbances in transitional subjects. Nevertheless, the nature of the disturbance, that is, the structure of the intruding elements should be only from a preceding or succeeding stage, and should themselves be predictable.

Flavell and Wohlwill (1969) have pointed out there may be two possible causes for these disturbances, if we conceive of the theory at the two levels of competence and performance. One form, at the competence level, would be caused by actual differential rates of formulation of the structures themselves. At the performance level there may be another form produced by different degrees of difficulty presented by the contextual demands of various tasks, even though they are structurally equivalent. For example, conservation of weight and volume are structurally identical with conservation of quantity. Successful judgments involve the same features, reversibility, compensation between inter-related variables, the identity of an object or substance persisting. Yet conservation of weight and volume typically appear between two and four years after conservation of quantity.

The construction and dissolution of stages, coupled with possible resistance of experiences give rise to *horizontal décalage*, the existence of acts atypical of the currently prevalent structure. It would therefore be naive to attempt validation of the theory by anticipating a total, unifying structure to the cognitive acts of any particular individual. Nevertheless

Piaget's adherence to structuralist explanations, and the stage theory which emerges from that orientation, should lead to reasonably confident predictions of predominant modes of cognition displayed by most individuals for most of the time. If it does not, if *décalage* exceeds *structure*, and heterogeneity is characteristic of most children's performances most of the time, Piaget's account lacks predictive validity, a fundamental attribute of any theory.

Studies which contribute to an assessment of the notion of *structure d'ensemble* may be divided into two types:

(i) those assessing the inter-correlation of individuals' performances on a variety of tasks derived from a Piagetian stage and/or reporting the presence or absence of expected behaviours, and

(ii) those reporting the presence of unexpected precocious behaviours.

In the following sections we shall examine some of these studies.

Homogeneity and heterogeneity: correlational evidence and absence of expected behaviours

The existence of studies reporting low correlations between measures of a particular operation have been referred to by many authors (e.g. Pascual-Leone, 1970; Sigel and Hooper, 1968). For illustration we shall concentrate upon a few more recent examples.

The stage of concrete operations is considered to be the first manifestation of truly logical thought, and its structure is described by the groupings which we have already discussed (Chapter 2). An important feature of this stage is the ability to classify objects using several dimensions at once; that is, in a contingency table such as that shown for the classification of pale, medium, and dark skinned men, women and children (p. 34). Simultaneously and on the basis of the same concrete operational structure, the child should be able to perform multiple seriation tasks, in which he can construct ordered sequences of graded objects, and can match two or more sequences (such as figures and walking sticks) even when some are presented in reverse order. Hamel (1974) gave a battery of multiple classification and multiple seriation tests to groups of children between the ages of five-and-a-half years and nine years. Correlations were found within the range +0.39 and +0.72.

In a further study Hamel employed 240 test items, covering classification, seriation, multiple classification and multiple seriation, with children representing the same age range. Analyses of variance showed a very considerable significant variation both within and between groupings. Furthermore, there was considerable evidence of task-specificity in the children's responses. The largest number of correct answers was given for task classification, followed by seriation, multiple classification, and multiple seriation respectively. The importance of contextual cues was suggested by the fact that most correct solutions were obtained if the task involved judgment on a colour dimension, and least if number was involved.

The vast majority of studies in cognitive development use cross-sectional data. A notable exception was that undertaken by Neimark (1975). The transition from concrete operations to formal operations was traced by assessing children aged between nine and twelve years for between three and four years. A variety of tests were used, amongst which were

(i) colour combinations, in which pairs of coloured sequences had to be identified giving every possible combination of any two of six colours,

(ii) presentation of digits, which required the subject to generate all the four digit sequences which use each of the numbers 1 to 4 once only, and

(iii) a correlational task in which an assessment of the probability of two events occurring together had to be assessed.

Neimark concluded that within each task there was evidence of a developmental sequence, suggesting a reasonable degree of concurrency (although combinations emerged slightly in advance of, and developed more quickly than, the other two tests). However test-retest correlations and between measures correlations were only of the order of +0.4. Of the fifty-eight children in her sample who scored at 'level 3' on combinations, twenty-four scored at 'level 0' on permutations, eight at 'level 1', nineteen at 'level 2' and seven at 'level 3'. The author considered the problem of how to define success on a task. She argued for a 'strong' criterion 'on the grounds that a stage . . . cannot be said to be attained until its component operations are integrated and fully generalizable'.

On those grounds it was concluded that various aspects of formal operations do not appear concurrently, and that full formal operations had not been achieved by the majority of the oldest group.

Performance on tests of formal operations was also assessed by Schwebel (1975). His sample of thirty men and thirty women had a mean chronological age of nineteen years, and were, on average, one standard deviation above the population mean on tests of mathematical and mental abilities. The Piagetian tests involved discovering the relationships of length, thickness and type of material to the flexibility of rods; the second to discover the law of moments with unequal weights and a balance; the third to predict the movements of a truck on an inclined plane, as a function of height, weight, and a counterbalancing weight. All of these are traditional Piagetian tasks which are soluble when formal operational structures generate hypothetico-deductive reasoning (Inhelder and Piaget, 1958), and the scoring procedures were as prescribed by their originators.

Intercorrelations between test performances ranged from 0.30 to 0.37. Of the thirty women in the sample, 27 per cent responded at the concrete level, 63 per cent at the lower formal, and 10 per cent at the upper formal level. The corresponding percentages for the men were 7 per cent concrete, 63 per cent lower formal, and 30 per cent upper formal, using two responses out of three as the criterion for success. Schwebel concluded that 'the three tasks appear to be relatively independent of each other' (p. 137).

Wason and Johnson-Laird (1972) also working in the field of formal operations cited similar evidence. Their work extensively analysed the nature of abstract reasoning, pointing out that there were a number of contextual factors which consistently misled the reasoner from a strictly logical conclusion. In so doing it cast some doubt on the adequacy of formal operations as an appropriate model. Twenty-four subjects were asked to imagine that they were postal workers. They were asked to discover whether the following rule had been violated: 'if the letter is sealed it has a five penny stamp on it'. The test material consisted of four envelopes arranged to show: the back of a sealed envelope, the back of an unsealed envelope, the front of an envelope with a fivepenny stamp, the front of an envelope with a fourpenny stamp on it. Subjects were asked to indicate which envelopes needed to be turned to test the rule. Under these 'concrete' conditions twenty-one subjects succeeded.

When the same logical task was presented in an 'abstract' form, with cards with letters and numbers, the subjects were less successful. Only two were able to test correctly the rule 'if the card has a "5" on one side it has a "D" on the other'.

In spite of complete identity of logical structure, subjects' abilities were apparently influenced by context as well as the possession of powers to employ the conditional rule. Whilst *horizontal décalage* could be invoked to explain this difference, such *ad hoc* explanation renders the presence of structure untestable.

An attempt to relate the structure of formal operations to the characteristics of adolescent personality development was undertaken by Blasi and Hoeffel (1974). These authors noted that, whilst Inhelder and Piaget (1958) recognised the influence of non-cognitive factors, they none the less assigned the development of formal structures as the principal influence on adolescent development. It was, therefore, necessary for Blasi and Hoeffel to attempt to establish the validity of the formal operational structure before proceeding. To this end they summarised a large number of studies covering many different samples, using various criteria for formal operations on tasks as diverse as *internal volume, rod flexibility, pendulums,* and *historical and geographical concepts*. Because of this diversity, comparisons were difficult, but, the authors asserted 'one conclusion seems unavoidable: a rather large percentage of individuals of normal intelligence and of average social background, not only at the age of adolescence, but also in adulthood, do not seem to function at the formal operational stage' (1974, p. 348).

Variations in estimates of the percentage of subjects in the formal operational stage ranged between 0 per cent to 80 per cent for subjects younger than eleven years; 0 per cent to 100 per cent between the ages of eleven and fourteen years; 10 per cent and 87 per cent between the ages of fifteen and eighteen years; and from 52 per cent to 100 per cent over the age of eighteen years. When the same test was applied to different samples the percentage varied from 0 per cent to 35 per cent.

These data suggest that the assignment to a particular stage seems to depend upon the task used as criterion, and the implication of structure is that it should not. However, Piaget (1972a) has elaborated reasons why, at the formal operational level, homogeneity is not expected. He suggests that two factors probably contribute to the observed heterogeneity:

  (i) that speed of acquisition varies from culture to culture, and

  (ii) in the second decade of life there is a much greater diversity of aptitude with age.

For these reasons 'our fourth period can no longer be characterized as a proper stage, but would already seem to be a structured advancement in the direction of specialization' (1972a, p. 9). In this respect it is quite different from the stage of concrete operations. It is worthy of note that to an extent (albeit an unspecified extent) Piaget appears to have modified the stage concept at this level, though in so doing he distinguishes it from concrete operations, to which the original concept still applies. His statement is also a clear acknowledgment of the influence of experience at this level, a feature to which he has given little emphasis.

Even in the concrete operational stage evidence of heterogeneity cannot disconfirm the theory however, for it will be recalled that a certain amount of heterogeneity is to be expected. Yet the studies we have cited cover the whole age range from five-and-a-half years to adolescence, and all used authentic Piagetian tests. For the notion of structure to remain credible we must assume either that all the subjects of these studies were in transitional states or were using material resistant to the prevailing structure.

Similar evidence of heterogeneity is to be found in the work of Piaget's own associates. In an experimental manipulation of training procedures for the conservation of continuous quantity (Inhelder *et al.*, 1974) thirty-four children between the ages of five and seven years were given tasks involving conservation of liquids and modelling clay. Fifteen children were categorised as 'non-conservers', but nineteen (more than half the group) were euphemistically labelled 'intermediate'. Of those, six failed the first task but succeeded on the second, nine gave mixed correct and incorrect answers on both tasks, and four were successful on the first but not the second task. Similar margins of 'intermediacy' are to be seen in most of the data they presented.

Of those studies which reported correlations between performances on different tests, all produced coefficients which were significant. To that extent associations between aspects of a structure have been established, and such results are often taken as confirmation of a *structure d'ensemble*. Yet none accounts for more than 50 per cent of the variance and we believe that Piaget's descriptions of stages leads us to expect much more coherent structures than these results suggest.

The weakness in all these studies, as we have already inferred, is that they do not seriously test the basic theoretical propositions. For various practical reasons children and adolescents are usually sampled from age groups. Yet the theory makes no claims that chronological age is particularly relevant except in the very loosest way. Flavell (1963) asserted: 'he (Piaget) cautions against an overliteral identification of *stage* with *age* and asserts that his own findings give rough estimates at best of the mean ages at which various stages are achieved . . .' (p. 20).

It is therefore possible that in each cohort there would be some who had already achieved full mastery of a stage, and others who were in various transition stages. For instance, if entry into Stage 2 is by means of three transition stages *a*, *b*, and *c*, then correlations would appear low if *developmentally* the sample was non-uniform. This is expressed in Table 4.1.

Table 4.1 Notional heterogeneity caused by transition phases

	Full stage 1	Intermediate stages			Full stage 2
		a	*b*	*c*	
Subject A	√	√	√	√	√
Subject B	√	√	√	√	X
Subject C	√	√	√	X	X
Subject D	√	√	X	X	X
Subject E	√	X	X	X	X

This table incorporates another aspect of the theory, that is, the orderly progression through transition stages *a, b* and *c*. Yet it is clear that in many studies this pattern is not manifest. In the Genevan study already cited (Inhelder *et al.*, 1974) there was an apparently random assortment of successes and failures.

We therefore conclude that there is, to say the least, an element of doubt raised by these studies as to the integrity of the theoretical model.

Possibly explanations of the studies cited above hinge upon the possibility that heterogeneity is the result of some, or all of the subjects being in transitional states. There are other studies for which this explanation will not suffice, in which markedly precocious behaviours have been reported.

Evidence of precocious behaviours

According to Genevan studies, early sensori-motor behaviour indicates that there is no concept of object constancy. When objects which have been on view are occluded the child's reaction suggests that he is no longer aware of their existence. Up to the age of about six months (sub-stages I to III) he will simply focus his attention elsewhere when an object is fully covered. During the following six months (sub-stage IV) he becomes able to recover the object in its usual place, that is if it is concealed again in the customary place. If it is concealed elsewhere, or occluded by a different object, he will fail. It is believed that it is not until the age of about eighteen months (sub-stage VI) that the child has a 'signifier' or personal symbolic representation which persists in the absence of the object. This development is acclaimed by Elkind and Sameroff (1970) as 'the most significant of Piaget's discoveries'.

In discussing this work, Bower (1974) recognised that Piaget's reasoning accounted for the observed behaviour, but put forward an alternative interpretation; that the infant *did* know that an object was under a cloth but did not know how to retrieve it. To determine which of these hypotheses was true it was necessary to find a measure of search behaviour which the infant could perform. Using changes in heart-rate and head and eye movements as estimators of surprise reaction Bower demonstrated that children who were expected to be in sub-stage II (2–4 months) appeared to possess object constancy. An object was placed on view, and was then concealed behind a screen. Reactions were then monitored when the screen was removed (a) to reveal the object, and (b) to reveal no object.

He maintained that 'these data . . . would seem to prove conclusively that quite young infants . . . know that objects still exist after they have been occluded . . .' (Bower, 1974, p. 189).

Bower suggested that the absence of gross motor behaviour by these infants was simply due to limited motor abilities. The fact that the observations of behaviours agreed with those made by Piaget, but that alternative explanations were offered for them we consider to be important. As we have already observed agreement in observations may too readily be taken as corroboration of the explanatory theory without systematic attempts to exclude alternatives.

Bryant's work on transitive inference (Bryant, 1974) has already been studied in Chapter 3. Whereas the structures required for this operation are not expected to be present before the stage of concrete operations, Bryant was able to demonstrate that, when errors due to memory load were eliminated, 88 per cent of a sample of five-year-olds could perform it.

The limitations of Piagetian questioning protocols were also raised in a study by Povey and Hill (1975). Fifty-six children between the ages of two years, four months and four years, ten months, were given concept acquisition tasks involving *specific concepts* (identifying pictures of objects), and *generic concepts* (selecting pictures which depict 'food' and 'people'). Half of the sample were also asked some Piagetian questions (given six cards depicting girl, lady, boy, lady, they were asked 'Are they all people?', 'Are there more ladies than people?' etc.)

Theory asserts that 'true concepts' are not possible at this age, as they require hierarchical classification with logical inclusion. These are determined by the groupings which structure the stage of concrete operations. Using Piagetian questions the authors found little evidence of the use of concepts, whereas their own material showed that most of the older children and many of the younger had formed specific concepts. Some of the older children were also competent with generic concepts.

An experiment similar to that by Povey and Hill was conducted by Harris in 1975. It explored the attainment of class inclusion with children between the ages of five and seven years. Harris investigated their ability to classify concepts (e.g. oak, ash, beech) under a superordinate class (tree), and to attribute the characteristics of that superordinate class to a new member by inference. That is, could the children infer that, if teak was also a tree, it must have the same attributes as the rest of the class? To eliminate the possibility that the children might use previously memorised information instead of reasoning the author employed nonsense words assigned to the classes *bird, house, aeroplane, man*. He concluded that the children could, indeed, infer attributes from class membership. Furthermore, the children were capable of identifying additional, non-essential attributes. Thus, when told that a nonsense word represented a red drink they could deduce that it was not milk. Harris identified the reasoning process as follows:

if *milk*, then *white*, $p.q$
not white $\bar{q}$
therefore not milk $\therefore \bar{p}$

This familiar inference is known as *modus tollendo tollens* and is generally considered part of the cognitive process of formal operations. Whilst Harris did not maintain that such reasoning would be spontaneously deployed by children of this age, the fact that such a structure was available and that logical behaviour could be elicited, casts further doubt on the Genevan structures.

These studies by Povey and Hill and by Harris both raise the issue of substituting everyday language for traditional Genevan procedures. This is something to which we shall return later in this chapter.

Precocious judgments were also reported by Gelman (1972). Children between the ages of two-and-a-half and four years were found able to conserve pattern-recognisable numbers, understand quantity changes caused by addition and subtraction, and understand the 'one unit' difference between the numbers 2 and 3. In a later series of experiments (Gelman and Tucker, 1975) children aged three, four and five years were studied for their ability to handle number-relevant and number-irrelevant transformations in tasks involving conservation of number. White cards with sets depicted by numbers of objects were exposed for intervals of 1, 5 and 60 seconds. The youngest children counted overtly, whereas the older ones did not, but none had any difficulty in estimating the number sets which were homogeneous. Only when mixed sets were employed (two mice and one soldier) did some children fail to perceive the identity of the set. Number-irrelevant transformations did not influence performance in most cases, although the authors were cautious in their conclusions as verbal responses suggested that many children felt more confident with homogeneous sets, and somehow felt mixed sets to be not quite equivalent. This study illustrates the problems of disentangling actual choice patterns from accompanying verbal commentary.

In a review of disconfirmatory evidence of the synchronous development of concrete operations (Brainerd, 1975) it was concluded that success was achieved on tasks involving seriation earlier than on tasks involving classification. Yet on theoretical grounds, and on the basis of empirical studies, Piaget refutes this (Piaget and Inhelder, 1964). In the light of what we have already said, there is a possibility that this apparent contradiction may be the result of adopting different criteria for assessing competence.

Consider a situation in which a child of five years never shows a particular operation, and is unable to demonstrate it even with training. He can be said to be without the necessary competence (or available structure). Another child, of eight years, may show clear indications of the operation on some occasions but not on others. Attempts to achieve uniformity across tasks may be partially successful, so this child does have the necessary competence, but lacks a complete automaton/performance system which applies the operation to all situations. Subsequently this system would become applicable to more and more situations. To adopt Flavell and Wohlwill's model would be to explain apparent contradictions as disagreements in the performances which are necessary to denote the presence of an underlying competence.

How are we to respond to studies such as we have surveyed? Do they seriously attack the validity of Piaget's claims? Brainerd (1973b) has argued that stage theories have enjoyed little support from psychologists generally because of a 'prima facie' inconsistency between the notion of a succession of qualitatively distinct behavioural states and the very continuous-looking data base that has accumulated over the years' (p. 349). By assuming that Piaget's description of structures is a description of competence, that is, of a coherent set of logical relationships from which cognitive behaviours are generated, we can attempt to render compatible the findings of the studies described above. Whereas, if we retain the expectation of homogeneity of performance we cannot.

If there is some complexity in the issue of homogeneity within a stage, there is more to be discovered in the notion of a sequence of stages. We shall now turn to this aspect of the theory.

The concept of stage sequence

In Chapter 3 we looked at typical studies of stage sequence, and made the point that they needed further scrutiny in order to clarify the model of stage which they employed. We now wish to return to this point.

Flavell (1971) argued that many studies betray a naive view of stages as consisting of inter-related behaviours which all emerge together as fully functioning repertoires. He represented this view schematically (Fig. 4.1a).

The diagram shows three sequential stages each represented by just one behaviour. The vertical axis represents the functional maturity of the behaviour, that is, the extent to which the behaviour is evoked in all appropriate circumstances. It can be seen from the figure that it does not admit of the acquisition of a stage, but represents an individual as either 'in' one stage or another. There is no period of transition. The change from Stage I to Stage II is denoted by the cessation of one behaviour and its replacement by another.

Whilst it may be argued that Flavell has set up a 'straw man' with this model, it will at least serve as a baseline from which more sophisticated models may develop.

A more subtle conception is portrayed in Figure 4.1b. This model conceives of a stage as involving the gradual acquisition of functional maturity. That is, the notion of a child being 'in' Stage I is now less useful, for the extent to which he will manifest 'appropriate' Stage I behaviours will depend not only upon the structure of Stage I, but also upon how far

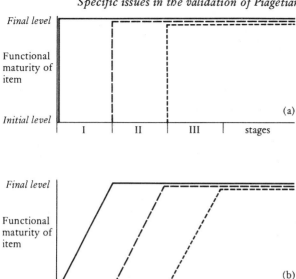

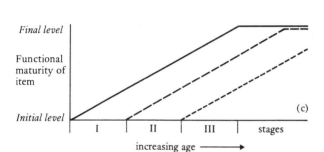

Figure 4.1 *Models of 'stage' (after Flavell, 1971)*

into the stage he has progressed. Progression entails the gradual extension of behaviours to more and more diverse experiences for which that structure is appropriate. The 'complete possession' of the stage, moreover, is now coincident with the onset of the following stage. Whereas, in the earlier model there was no period of transition, in this model the whole of the stage constitutes a process of development.

Figure 4.1c illustrates a further progression. In this model there would be little utility in describing a child as *in* a stage, but one could describe him as exhibiting the first indications of the functions of that stage. In so doing there would be no implication that previous stages had been completed.

Piaget's own description of the fluctuations in performance which accompany transition between stages would seem to rule out the first model. Flavell comments, perhaps regretfully, that 'It lends a meaning to "stage" that is conceptually clear, theoretically strong, operationally useful. . . . Unfortunately that developing system we call the child just does not seem to conform to it' (1971, p. 10).

By reference to Piaget's own description Flavell concludes that the second model best represents the Genevan view.

> A stage thus comprises both a level of *preparation*, on the one hand, and of *achievement*, on the other. For example, in the case of formal operations, the stage of preparation would be the entire period from 11 to 13-14 years and the achievement would be the state or level (*palier*) of equilibrium which is obtained at the end of that period (Piaget, 1955, p. 35, trans. and cited by Flavell, 1971, p. 10).

Thus, during the development of a stage a particular operation will slowly assume generality and stability, and by the end of the stage it will have achieved it.

We have already seen that the heterogeneity of operations discovered in various studies makes even this model difficult to sustain. To maintain that a child is in a particular stage is not particularly helpful unless you know on what tasks the assessment was made, and whether the tasks were adequate to make assumptions of a generalised ability. It may well be the case that in some situations a child will produce behaviours characteristic of a given stage, but not in others; that is, the operation is at a relatively low level of functional maturity. Flavell (op. cit.) in supporting the third model of stage, goes further than this, arguing that there is also good reason to believe that cognitive behaviours continue to develop and be utilised long after the stage to which they belong has ceased to be adequate to describe the individual's mode of functioning.

> Consider a random example of a sensory-motor acquisition: the ability to discover new means for achieving a concrete goal through active experimentation, e.g. to discover that a stick can be used to fetch an out-of-reach object. . . . It is surely true that this sort of ability continues

to be refined and perfected long after the child has left the sensory-motor period (Flavell, 1971, p. 12).

It is difficult to imagine that anyone could disagree with this view, although it may be that the heavy emphasis on sequential development through stages has led to its being paid scant attention. The implication that Flavell draws is that reference to an emergent stage is best conceived as an idealised description of a structure, the presence of which is indicated by emergent functions of that structure.

To describe this structure which underlies the acts is not, in this case, to offer a description of a structure which we will expect to find in all, or most, of the individual's behaviour; but of logical structure which, over a period of time, the individual will operationalise in various contexts. In other words, the stage model is a competence model.

From the studies indicating heterogeneity in children's performance we have concluded that stage must be conceived as characterised by *structure d'ensemble* only at the competence level, and by emergent functions at the performance level. As a corollary of the latter we recognise that at any particular point in time a child may be simultaneously developing functions belonging to two or more stage structures. Thus, the Piagetian theory of an invariant sequence of stages is interpreted as an invariant sequence of logical structures, indicated by the strictly sequential emergent functions of each in turn. However, it will be recalled that in Chapter 3 we examined some cross-cultural studies which seemed to cast doubt upon any interpretation of a universal and invariant sequence. The problem of validation has now become a very complex one. If we wish to determine whether competence A always precedes competence B we must look to see whether there is *always* evidence of emergent functions of A before those of B. Individual instances of B before A are now of no consequence, for we do not expect a full repertoire of A-type behaviours before any B-type behaviours. We have already alluded to a number of methodological and contextual variables which may account for such reversals, and in a later section of this chapter we shall explore them more fully. So we now have a model which may render much of the evidence compatible, but it is an extremely difficult one to validate.

Flavell's third model also enables us to conceive of the

child's level of ability in terms of an underlying competence, and the extent to which a given task may contain clues which elicit it, and the extent to which it may be spontaneously utilised in a relevant context. We shall return to this issue later in this chapter.

Concurrent developments within the stage

So far we have taken a single behaviour as an exemplar of a stage, in order to discuss the relationship between stages. Another aspect of a stage structure is that all the logical constituents emerge and operate in unison (although we do not necessarily expect behaviours based upon them to do so). Flavell and Wohlwill (1969) point out that Piaget has placed a heavy demand upon his theory by maintaining this. A *structure d'ensemble* would still be recognisable within a pattern of operations which each developed along a different time schedule. To determine a unison of competences presents us with a similar problem to that of testing the assumption of invariant sequence, namely, how are we to pursue it, given the unpredictable and ill-defined relationship between competence and performance?

Flavell and Wohlwill (1969) attempted to clarify this relationship. They assumed two determinants of a child's performance on a task: A, the structures embodied in the task (equivalent to competence), and B, the operating rules which the child needed in order to process the information from the task and produce a result (performance).

Three factors were postulated as jointly involved in determining performance:

- P_a, the probability that the operation functions in the child
- P_b, the probability attached to a task of the information being correctly processed, assuming that P_a is greater than 0
- K, the weight attached to P_b for a particular child.

It will be seen that two of these factors relate to the individual child (P_a and K), and one to the task (P_b).

For the sake of simplicity K was assumed to vary from 0 at an early phase to 1.0 at a phase when the stage is fully developed and generalised. At this latter point the influence of the task attributes would be very small. Thus an equation for the probability (P) that a child solved a task was suggested to be:

$$P = P_a \times P_b^{1-K}$$

The interest in this highly speculative endeavour derives from the authors' attempts to use it to describe how an operation may develop, and to speculate upon the degree of concurrency which might be expected between operations.

Initial phase

$P_a = 0$: The child fails all problems demanding the operation.

Phase 2

P_a changes from 0 to 1: Competence present.
K is assumed to remain close to 0 as contextual variables are likely to be maximal, and because the abstraction of relevant information is dependent upon establishing the operation.

Thus in the middle of this phase ($P_a = 0.5$) with a task of medium difficulty ($P_b = 0.5$):
$P = 0.25$: the child will probably fail 3 times out of 4.

Phase 3

$P_a = 1$: Period of stabilisation and consolidation.
Success will be variable, particularly at the beginning of this phase, because of the varying levels of task demands (i.e. P_b). Subsequently, as K approaches 1, $1 - K$ becomes very small.

Final phase

$P_a = 1$: as previously established.
$1 - K$ becomes very small as K approaches 1: the operation can now be applied to almost any task. Therefore unless P_b is very low, i.e. the task is very difficult:
$P = 1$: the child will succeed on all tasks.

We have no wish to minimise the problems inherent in such an attempt at quantification, nor have its authors. There are problems relating to the size of domain over which a parameter might apply, quite apart from the empirical difficulties of establishing the values of coefficients. Nevertheless the model offers an extension of Piagetian ideas taking into account variables which, as we have shown, are implicated (or appear to be implicated) in Genevan studies.

With respect to the interrelationships between operationally equivalent tasks this model has some interesting implications. Those studies which have correlated performances between such tasks, and have led to conclusions that low correlation coefficients denote absence of *structure d'ensemble* (e.g. Neimark, 1975) may now be interpreted differently. During the Initial phase overall failure would produce low correlations because of lack of variance. In Phase 2, when P_a had intermediate value, correlations would again be low because of oscillations and inconsistencies in response. As individual variability diminishes in Phase 3 (i.e. when P_a and K approach unity) the influence of the task variable, P_b, should manifest itself so that items of equal value should be successfully processed with equal frequency, and correlations should be high. Furthermore those items with more or less difficulty should exhibit Guttman-type patterns which would reflect their relatively high or low weightings. Finally, correlations should again diminish due to lack of variance as overall success is achieved.

This speculatory development could be used to explain some of the correlational data which we cited earlier. Its weakness, in our view, lies in ascribing variations to two independent factors, lack of variance and loadings on P_b. It would seem to us that, if this model is to be pursued, it would be desirable to abandon correlational analyses in favour of scalogram analyses.

In support of their model Flavell and Wohlwill presented the results of a study by Uzgiris in which assumed values of P_a, P_b and K were matched to the response patterns of children in Grades 1 to 6 (Uzgiris, 1962). The authors concluded that 'when we assign Ss in the various grades to these phases, based on their response patterns, a very consistent pattern emerges' (1969, p. 117)—and—'Altogether, these data provide a certain amount of empirical support for the adequacy of the model we have outlined, sufficient at least to warrant further research . . .' (ibid., p. 118).

The authors make no stronger claim than that, and properly so. The fitting of data to the model was a *post hoc* venture, and the coefficient introduced as P_b for the various tasks appears to be based on nothing stronger than the expectation that conservation of substance would precede conservation of weight. The assurance that 'iterative procedures . . . would no doubt . . . improve upon these approximations' (ibid., p. 117) is undoubtedly true, but a test of the model would require the confirmation of predictions generated from it rather than the *post hoc* fitting of data to it.

As this model was put forward over a decade ago, it is perhaps surprising that it has not been pursued more vigorously. In any case we doubt that it could be seen as support for the Piagetian notion of stage. As the postulated structures cannot readily be discerned in behaviour, and, as we shall see in the following section, they may not be there when behaviours suggest that they are, we are in some doubt as to how the concept of stage may be validated. Problems associated with the search for competence will be our next theme.

Empirical problems in studying competence

We have already seen that Piaget makes a range of claims about various sequences and synchronies in the development of operations. To test these claims it is necessary to have a set of performance criteria by which to judge the presence or absence of these operations and their earliest data of emergence. Note that the age of emergence *per se* is of no theoretical importance. Piaget does not assign particular acquisitions to particular ages on any theoretical basis. However, to test the claim that operation A precedes operation B it is necessary to establish that operation A can be found in the absence of B and that B can never be found in the absence of A. We thus need to identify the minimal acceptable evidence of the earliest manifestations of operations A and B.

The search for these sequential acquisitions may be expedited by giving tests of operational competence to samples of children of various ages or by means of training studies (see Chapter 5). In either case the aforementioned criteria are still necessary, in the former case to judge performance on the tests and in the latter to judge the effects of training.

Interpreting performances on tasks

In interpreting a child's performance on a task we run the risk of making one of two types of error, a false positive error or a false negative error (see Table 4.2).

Table 4.2 Error types in relating performance to competence

	Success on task	Failure on task
Child has underlying competence	Performance correlated with competence	False negative error. Failure due to factor other than lack of competence
Child has not underlying competence	False positive error. Success due to factor other than competence	Performance correlated with competence

A false negative error involves concluding that the child is without competence when in fact he has competence. A false positive error involves assuming the child has competence when in fact he has not. In assessing performance on tests of underlying competence it must be established that there is only one source of failure—a lack of competence, and only one route to success—that deriving from the appropriate competence. We have already explored some of the problems in meeting this demand (see the discussion of Bryant's work in Chapter 3). In what follows we examine this ostensibly psychometric problem in greater detail and show it to have far reaching consequences for the empirical evaluation of Piaget's theory.

False negative errors

A number of Piaget's critics argue that he makes large-scale false negative errors in interpreting children's performances on his task. That is to say he underrates children's competence (Brainerd, 1977a; Donaldson, 1978; Gelman, 1972).

There is a number of sources of false negative errors. The child could be inattentive, might not comprehend the instructions or might not remember the instructions. These would be errors originating in the stimulus demands of the task. Another source of error lies in the response demands of the task. The child might be perfectly able to cope with the task intellectually but the response we demand might be beyond his capabilities. For example, in researching babies' memories we may hide things under cushions. If the baby does not move the cushion in his search, we could conclude that the baby has no memory of the hidden object. He might have a perfectly good memory of the object's location but be incapable of getting to the cushion, or moving it if he gets there. Additionally we are all familiar with being able to understand a concept or issue and not be able to express our understanding of it. If a verbal account is demanded we will be judged to lack comprehension and our judge will have made a false negative error—unless, of course, the capacity for verbal expression is a justifiable part of the criterion for comprehension.

To show that such errors are possible does not establish that Piaget actually makes them. That he is guilty of this has to be shown in specific instances. We have already described Bryant's work on transitive inference in this respect (see Chapter 3). Further evidence of Piaget's propensity for false negative errors is extensive. Studies of the development of object permanence are a particularly rich source. According to Piaget (1955) object permanence is one of the most significant attainments of the sensori-motor period. The concept that objects exist independently of our perceptions and actions is constructed. It is Piaget's view that the very young infant has no appreciation of the objectivity of things. His view rests on his interpretation of observations of infant responses to the movement and hiding of objects. Piaget's observations have been replicated by many students of infant behaviour (see Gratch, 1975, 1976 for reviews). Piaget offers a competence model of the futile search behaviours of infants. Underlying such behaviour is the lack of a sense of the permanence of objects. Later, goal oriented search strategies are taken to be premised on the infants' possessing such a sense of object constancy.

Recent studies however imply that the very young infant has such knowledge. The attention requirements, memory requirements and response requirements of tasks have been shown to be implicated in the child's failure.

It is unlikely that infants will initiate successful search behaviours if they are not attending to the object when it goes missing. Gratch *et al.* (1974) showed that infants who err in search showed persistence in attending to a location associated with successful previous search rather than attending to the new 'hide' i.e. the new location was not attended to in the first place. Cornell (1978) made video tape recordings of children's gaze during search tasks. The very small proportion of successful searches recorded seemed due to the infants' tendency to show poor attention. Many of them turned their eyes to look at the experimenter's face or twisted to look at Mum.

Other studies have shown that memory limitations influence performance on object constancy tests (Bower, 1967; Gratch, 1975; Harris, 1973, 1974). Any increase in delay of responding, induced by the experimenter, is associated with an increase in futile search behaviours, or with surprise responses interpreted as arising from the infant anticipating a novel event rather than an event stored in memory. Thus performance on object permanence tests may reflect difficulties posed by memory limitations rather than a lack of the constructed constancy of objects. We do not wish to maintain that the development of memory and the development of object constancy are two entirely separate issues. They are not. The growth of memory obviously requires the development of coherent, permanent representations of events and processes. The point here is that under some conditions of short delay and rapt attention children behave as if they have object constancy and under longer delays and inattention they do not. Without a precise definition of what counts as object constancy we cannot discuss whether a child has this important acquisition or not.

Entirely similar problems in which stimulus and response factors can be shown at work generating false negative errors may be cited in reviews of the Piagetian concepts of egocentricity (Borke, 1978; Flavell, 1974); conservation of number (Gelman, 1972); pre-operational structures (Siegel, 1978); and formal operational structures (Blasi and Hoeffel, 1974), several of which we have already cited. Gelman (1972) noted that Piaget's test of number conservation was, 'at a minimum, a test for logical capacity, the control of attention, correct semantics and estimation skills' (1972, p. 89). Any error on the part of the child in terms of attention, semantics or estimation skills meant failure on the task. Failure on the task, in Piagetian terms, is attributed to a lack of logical capacity and would, under these circumstances be a false negative error.

Reducing false negative errors

It is necessary to identify the possible sources of false negative errors, demonstrate that these sources do in fact operate, and then design control conditions in testing to eliminate their effects. This is very easily said but proves extremely difficult to do. The problems that ensue and their implications for evaluating the theory are discussed in the following sections.

The use of non-verbal techniques

Piaget's tasks are cloaked in language. Instructions and questions are presented verbally and the child is generally asked not only to make a judgment but to give a verbal justification of that judgment. Many of Piaget's critics have commented that the language demands of the tasks are in excess of the operational demand being tested (Braine, 1959; Flavell, 1963; Siegel, 1978). Such excess demands would lead to false negative errors in judgments of the child's operational competence.

For example, the existence of the pre-operational stage is marked by the absence of certain cognitive operations such as conservation and class inclusion. Tests for these operations require that the child has a grasp of relational terms such as 'more' or 'bigger than'. But we know from other studies that children exhibit significant limitations in their comprehension of these terms (Clark, 1973; Donaldson and Balfour, 1968 for example). Clearly, in some respects the possession of an intellectual process is not entirely independent of appropriate linguistic manifestations and Flavell has warned that 'there is probably a point beyond which stripping a concept of its verbal-symbolic accouterments makes of it a different, lower order concept, or even no concept at all . . .' (1963, p. 436). The crucial question however is specifically in what way are we to take the 'verbal-symbolic accouterments' of a concept as necessary criteria for judging the possession of the concept? The only substantive area to seek resolution of a criterion problem is within the theory which generated the problem. In this respect the theory is quite unequivocal. In Piaget's theory language is neither the source of cognitive development nor the means of representing cognitive structure. Cognition precedes language (Sinclair, 1969). For Piaget, 'language behaviour is . . . treated as a dependent variable with cognition as the independent variable' (Flavell, 1963, p. 271). This is the case for all stages of development. Whilst in the formal operational period language is increasingly recognised as a potent source of input (Inhelder and Piaget, 1958), Piaget has made it quite clear that the representational levels of the concrete and formal operational stages are identical and neither is linguistic (Piaget, 1967). Thus there is every justification, from the standpoint of the theory, to strip away the 'verbal accouterments' of concepts both at the stimulus and response end of the tasks used to assess operational attainments. To do otherwise, to demand, for example, reasons for judgments, is to build in false negative errors from the point of view of the theory. The Genevans are perfectly aware of this problem (Piaget, 1929; Inhelder and Piaget, 1958) but generally seem to ignore it and indeed demand attention to justifications of responses given. For example, Inhelder and Sinclair (1969) suggest that, 'special attention should be paid to the child's justification of his answers . . .' (p. 5).

In direct contravention of this precept, but apparently more in keeping with Piaget's stance on the relationship between language and thought, large numbers of researchers have minimised the verbal trappings of cognitive development studies. They have reduced the complexity of instructions, frequently avoided the need for verbally expressed questions and abandoned the demand for justifications of judgments. These non-verbal methods (or more properly 'minimally verbal' methods since none are strictly non-verbal) have been extensively reviewed by Miller (1976) and in what follows we have drawn heavily on this work.

There seem to be three major types of non-verbal method; namely, motivated choice responses, instrumental choice responses and the use of surprise as a response. Under motivated choice conditions the outcome of the child's choice is considered to be informed by self-interest. Mehler and Bever (1967) published the first of such studies. Children from two years, six months upwards were presented with two rows of candy each containing four items in horizontal correspondence (see Fig. 4.2). They were asked to choose the row of candy they would like to eat. They were then presented with the distribution shown in stage two and asked to choose on the same basis. Almost 100 per cent of the children of

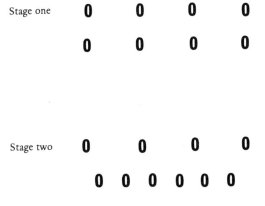

Figure 4.2   *Layout of candy (after Mehler and Bever, 1967)*

two-and-a-half chose the six sweets rather than the four spread out and the authors concluded that this was evidence that children of this age possessed the notion of conservation because a perceptual distribution had not misled them about judgments of quantity. There are several points of interest about this study. The first is that it is not a test of conservation at all since the transformation involves additional elements. Second, the youngsters' responses are open to a number of interpretations: they might choose on the basis of density rather than extension for example. Third, it has evidently proved very difficult to replicate. Most interesting however, is that children of four years of age were more likely than the youngest group to choose the longer line containing fewer sweets. As Miller points out, 'Although the choice of six candies over four can hardly be taken as evidence of conservation, selection of the row of four as the one to eat would seem to be striking evidence of non-conservation' (1976, p. 409).

Instrumental choice response studies involve training the child to make choices on the basis of reinforcement contingencies and a critical choice is then embedded in a conservation test. Braine (1959) used this technique to explore children's capacity to solve three-term transitive inference problems. He found children were capable of solving these problems two years younger than Piaget had suggested. Braine's conclusions have been subject to extensive criticism by Smedslund (1963, 1965). The argument between Braine and

Smedslund seems to mirror, in many important respects, the debate between Bryant and various Genevan proponents. It was Smedslund's view that the children Braine used solved his problem by processes other than transitivity; i.e. he claimed Braine to be making false positive errors. Since then the three-term transitive inference problem has been shown to be inherently flawed in respect of its demands for logical competence and it appears necessary to use at least five terms in the series (Bryant, 1974). The general point raised here is that under the constraints of instrumental conditioning procedures, tasks are used which fail to assess critical features of Piagetian operations (such as reversibility) or which are essentially different from the Piagetian task being examined.

Some experimenters avoid demanding any kind of instrumental response from the child. This is done by monitoring the child for 'surprise' reactions. It is argued that surprise must indicate an unconfirmed expectancy and the expectancy is taken to be premised on some underlying cognitive structure (Charlesworth, 1964, 1969). Gelman (1972) for example, showed that on responding to quantity judgments, children of two-and-a-half to three years of age were surprised by the covert addition or subtraction of elements but not by changes in spatial distribution. This was taken to imply that children had a sense of quantity-relevant and quantity-irrelevant processes and built expectations accordingly. In this sense Gelman concluded that they had an appreciation of the conservation of number. But Gelman's task differs in many important respects from Piaget's. Her set sizes were very small (two or three elements), there was minimal use of quantitative terms and an absence of a typical conservation transformation. The problem, once again, is whether the essential nature of the task is different from Piaget's task.

There are more general problems with the notion of surprise as an index. We may have an expectation but not show surprise at its violation (for all the same reasons that we can be tricked, fooled or misled by authority figures in experimental settings). Alternatively, for a surprise reaction to be a true indication of conservation the routine must produce a change which a conserver and only a conserver could find surprising. Miller (1976) shows that some studies have presented children with changes so massive that everyone might find the result a surprise or at least a thrill.

Following Miller (1976) we have seen that the use of non-verbal techniques in the assessment of the presence or absence of Piagetian operations raises as many problems as it solves. Whilst it offers a theoretically justifiable means of obtaining the minimally acceptable evidence of the earliest possible manifestation of operations it is clear that in many cases the child's response is open to more than one interpretation. This of course can be amended by suitable experimental design. More seriously the question is raised whether these procedures are testing a Piagetian concept at all (cf. our remarks on the Mehler and Bever study) or whether they are presenting a very much simpler version of a Piagetian task (cf. our remarks on Gelman's study and later discussion of Pascual-Leone, Chapter 6).

For these reasons it is Miller's (1976) view that non-verbal techniques have contributed little to the assessment and modification of Piaget's theory. Many non-verbal techniques show an earlier date of emergence of operations than Piaget's standard tests but are open to so many methodological criticisms as to be irrelevant to the theory. Other non-verbal techniques show results similar to Piaget's. These are taken to offer strong support to Piaget. If tasks such as Gelman's (1972) show an earlier emergence than Piaget's versions, they raise a fundamental problem for the theory. It becomes questionable if there is any point in postulating emergent factors in development. As Braine has observed, 'If "age of emergence" is *merely* a function of response requirements then the concept of emergence is less useful than a structural analysis of response requirements . . . concept of emergence obstructs psychological analysis' (1968, p. 187).

The notion of 'earliest date of emergence' has been pushed to its logical conclusion by some authors who search for inborn intellectual processes. Bryant (1974) for example, argues that this is a necessary construct to account for the use of relative perceptual codes in very early infancy. Epistemologically such a claim is nativist in form and as such is a serious challenge to Piaget's fundamental philosophical stance. A flurry of studies of the perceptual coding processes of neonates is under way but evidently seems to offer little conclusive evidence (Wallace, 1976).

Finally, with respect to the 'age of emergence' studies, Trabasso's work (see Chapter 3) using non-verbal techniques has shown an earlier date of emergence of transitive inference together with a radically different view of the cognitive processes at work. Trabasso's work is not beyond criticism however. It will be recalled that under Trabasso's training schemes, subjects build an image of the series and then use direct read-out procedures to answer questions from it. Processes of transitive inferential reasoning do not seem to be at work. This however could be an artefact of the training procedures used. Certainly at some stage in development people do use logical necessity to justify responses to transitive inference problems and a theory of cognitive development would have to give some account of how this came about. This critical point apart, Trabasso has taken a different view of how to progress in our understanding of cognitive development. His view entails studying mental processes rather than ascertaining the presence or absence of particular operations.

'Judgments' versus 'judgments and explanations'

We have already noted that Piagetians demand from their subjects explanations of their judgments. We have also shown that such a demand builds in to their data false negative errors from the point of view of their own theory. This argument has been developed most extensively by Brainerd (1973c) and Siegel (1978). Subsequently Brainerd has shown that the two techniques (i.e. demanding 'judgments' or demanding 'judgments plus explanations') reveal different effects when used to assess the sequential development of operations in the concrete operational stage (Brainerd, 1977a).

Piagetians suggest that a number of operations develop synchronously in this stage. This proposition is often tested by setting up the null hypothesis that the probability of finding operation A is no different from that of finding operation B in a sample of children. The presence of these operations is then assessed using standard Piagetian tests in which judgments and explanations are demanded. Such studies have been compared with others using identical tests but without requiring explanations of subjects' judgments. (Brainerd and Hooper, 1975; Papalia and Hooper, 1971.) It seems that the null hypothesis is accepted when 'judgments plus explanations' are demanded and frequently rejected when judgments only are used as criteria. That is, the synchrony predicted by Piaget is found using Genevan criteria and missing using non-Genevan (i.e. 'judgments only') criteria. Thus our view of synchrony within the concrete operational stage rests on which criterion we choose. We have already established that the 'judgments only' criterion is more consonant with Piaget's theory. Recently Brainerd (1977a) has shown the 'judgments only' criterion to be psychometrically more acceptable because it can be shown to be associated with a lower likelihood of either falsely accepting or falsely rejecting the null hypothesis. Thus Piaget's theory predicts within-stage synchrony and the criteria used for the identification of operations bias the findings in the direction of prediction. The 'judgment plus explanation' criterion, suspect both on theoretical and psychometric grounds, masks within-stage asynchrony.

Using hints to reduce false negative errors

It is conceivable that a subject may have the underlying competence necessary to perform a particular task but that the instructions do not evoke the knowledge pertinent to the problem. The task demands may be unclear or misleading. It is reasonable, under these circumstances, to hypothesise that this competence could be elicited by hints on the pertinence of various strategies. To give someone a hint is not to instruct the person. A hint can be useful only to those in possession of sufficient competence to make sense of it. Thus the use of hints could reduce the incidence of false negative errors by eliciting manifestations of competence otherwise obscured by ambiguous instructions.

The procedure is well illustrated in a recent study by Danner and Day (1977). They found it remarkable that so few adults perform well on tests of formal operations and speculated that one source of difficulty is that, in the usual format, tests for formal operations are extremely 'open ended'. That is to say, only the vaguest invitations are extended to find out, for example, what influences the rate of swing of a pendulum. They hypothesised that formal operational competence would be more in evidence if it were made clearer to subjects quite what was demanded of them in these tasks.

Their subjects were three groups of twenty, aged ten, thirteen and seventeen years respectively. Each subject was presented individually with three formal operations tasks; the flexibility of rods and the pendulum problems (Inhelder and Piaget, 1958), and the spinning wheel task (Case, 1974). The tasks were presented in the order rods, spinning wheel, pendulum. On the flexibility of rods problem the subject was invited to 'find out what makes differences in bending', on the spinning wheel problem to 'find out what influences the amount of time a marble will stay on a spinning wheel' and on the pendulum problem to 'find out what makes differences in how fast weights go back and forth'. Each task was presented in the traditional open-ended way and after trying each of the first two tasks a set of structured hints was given for a repeat performance of the task. The series of hints was gone through until the subject identified and tested all the variables in the task, or saw the experimenter do so. Each task involved four such variables. So the procedure was:

- Open ended attempt at flexibility of rods problem.
- Hint guided attempt at flexibility of rods problem.
- Open ended attempt at spinning wheel problem.
- Hint guided attempt at spinning wheel problem.
- Open ended attempt at pendulum problem.

A series of five prompts was arranged and given as necessary. In the first prompt the experimenter merely named any variable the subject had not tested and then asked him to test it. This was followed first by giving a verbal rule on testing variables, second the rule plus an example was given, third a direct instruction was given to test each variable in turn and finally the testing of all four variables was demonstrated. The number of variables tested under each condition was noted.

The important comparison was of unaided performance on task one with unaided performance on task three. As their criterion for judging formal operational status Danner and Day chose the identification and testing of three out of four variables. On this basis, unaided performance on task one showed results perfectly consistent with other studies of formal operations. None of the ten-year-olds performed at an acceptable level whilst 45 per cent and 55 per cent of the thirteen- and seventeen-year-olds respectively did so. Unaided performance on task three showed the effect of hints on tasks one and two. Under these circumstances 25 per cent of the ten-year-olds, 85 per cent of the thirteen-year-olds and 95 per cent of the seventeen-year-olds performed at a formal operational level. Under the effect of hints the performance of many subjects showed a marked transition to the formal operational level. Thus 5 of the 20 ten-year-olds, 8 of 11 thirteen-year-olds and 9 of 9 seventeen-year-olds made such a transition.

Immediate problems in interpreting this study are first, was the effect due to practice rather than prompt and second, was the 'hint' really an 'instruction' and therefore the study not one of present competence but the acquisition of competence?

In respect of the first point, Danner and Day carried out a study in which effects of practice were controlled. They used two groups of seventeen-year-olds and the test described above. One group had the routines as described whilst the other group had the routines without prompts. The first group exhibited all the effects of the initial study whilst the second group showed no improvement. The effect of practice seemed negligible.

Does a hint constitute instruction? The authors show that the effects of hints are radically different at different ages. The ten-year-olds got significantly more hints and made significantly less progress. Unfortunately there is no analysis of the effect of different hints. The first hint seems vague enough to avoid the charge of instruction:

1. The experimenter named any variable the subject had not tested and asked him to test it (Danner and Day, 1977, p. 1602).

The second hint, however, was a direct verbal instruction:

2. Verbal rule: The subject was given the following rule: 'A good way to find out what makes a difference in (bending/how long a marble will stay on a spinning wheel/how fast the weights go back and forth) is to make sure that everything is the same except the one thing you are testing' (ibid.).

The third hint was to give the above rule together with an example of its use. These certainly look like instructions and it is possible that the ten-year-olds made less of them because they simply knew less about rods, spinning wheels and pendulums. Variables cannot be tested without being identified and they cannot be identified without a considerable knowledge of the phenomena *per se*.

The criterion for deciding whether a subject is operating at a formal level is open to criticism. Danner and Day chose the ability to identify and test three of the four task variables as the mark of the formal operator. This is something of a pragmatic decision. The authors wanted, 'to avoid underestimating our subjects' competence . . .' (ibid., p. 1603). That is they sought to avoid false negative errors not only by the use of hints but by a somewhat arbitrary use of scoring procedures. The identification and testing of variables is not a sufficient criterion to be judged a formal operator. Additionally the identification of more rather than fewer variables does not seem to be a crucial or emergent cognitive advance.

The fundamental problem with the use of hints however, seems to hinge on the relationship between the hints and the underlying competence which is being assessed. The point is not whether a hint is an instruction but whether the nature and sequencing of the hints is informed by a description of the competence we seek to make manifest, or by an hypothesis about the obstruction we imagine the hint will remove. For such studies to achieve their objectives it is not enough that they replace the risk of false negative errors with the risk of false positive errors. This is likely if hints are simply *ad hoc* instructions and demonstrations. First, the hints must be generated from the theory. Second, they must match the perceived competence of the subject. To facilitate this the theory must provide a clear and operational definition of pertinent cognitive processes. This definition must then be assumed to be true for the generation of the hints so that the earliest date of emergence of these processes can be ascertained. It is evident that Piaget's theory does not provide such workable descriptions and studies using hints are likely to remain *ad hoc* in nature until relevant conceptual work is undertaken. It is noteworthy that a similar point was found to be at issue in the literature on the age of emergence of transitive inferential reasoning processes.

False positive errors

Just as various irrelevant aspects of the demands of a task might defeat a child and lead us to underestimate his competence, so it is equally conceivable that the child could succeed on a task by means other than those deriving from the operation under test. The child might guess appropriate responses or develop correct judgments from alternative reasoning processes. Under these circumstances we are likely to make false positive errors about the child's competence. This charge is often made by Piagetians when commenting on those studies challenging Genevan findings (Smedslund, 1963; Youniss and Furth, 1973, for example). In the following section we take a closer look at this defence and its implications for subsequent research.

In Chapter 3 we described de Boysson-Bardies and O'Regan's criticism of the work of Bryant and Trabasso. Briefly, their point was that the youngsters could be using an end point labelling strategy to solve Bryant and Trabasso's 'inference' problem. Similar criticisms have been made by Youniss and Furth (1973). Referring to Bryant and Trabasso (1971), these authors concluded that,

> here we have no more than a perceptual consistency; children were working with arbitrary relations among differently coloured rods. To be parsimonious their subjects can be said to have performed consistently in judging new pairs in an organised system dictated by the old, overlearned pairs (1973, p. 315).

Youniss and Furth then suggested that it is possible to control for this type of irrelevant strategy by making refinements to the stimuli and their order of presentation. In the five-term series, *A B C D E*, Bryant and Trabasso's routine was to train on pairs *AB, BC, CD* and *DE* and to test on pair *BD*. As we saw in Chapter 3 success on this may be interpreted as sublogical reasoning making use of images. To control for this, Youniss and Dennison (1971) showed *BD* after comparison with other rods but not with the middle term *C*. Murray and Youniss (1968) showed $B > C = D$; $B = C > D$ and $B > C > D$ and asked for judgments about *BD*. In these studies the age of emergence of transitive inference corresponded to that found in Piaget's own studies.

The first point to be made about this kind of study is that it does not demonstrate that children actually do use irrelevant strategies. The data are perfectly consistent with explanations derived from assumptions about logical or sub-logical strategies. The second is that whilst the controls used against the possibility of irrelevant strategies appear to preclude them,

the procedures used present problems sufficiently different
from the originals to raise doubts about whether they are
controls or different tasks presenting a different kind of
demand. To delete the middle term is to present a problem
which might not be soluble by means of a transitive inference
and Murray and Youniss's (1968) study might be interpreted
as showing that children have more difficulty with three term
series containing symmetrical relationships than those with
asymmetrical relationships. Clearly, the criterion problem is
at issue again. As Braine pointed out

> if one seeks to state an age at which a particular type of
> response develops, the only age which is not completely
> arbitrary is the earliest age at which this type of response
> can be elicited using the simplest experimental procedures
> (1968, p. 187).

The Genevans are driven to this kind of research by making
claims about the serial acquisition of various processes. Seriation, for example, is considered a pre-requisite for transitivity
(Piaget, Inhelder and Szeminska, 1960). Thus any developmental re-location of the emergence of transitivity demands a
similar re-location of earlier contributing processes. If dates
of emergence are functions of *ad hoc* variations of task parameters there is little hope of evaluating the theory's claims.
Finally, the defenders of Piaget have never taken irrelevant
strategies seriously. They have been postulated and shown to
be consistent with the data they are taken to explain, but
they have never been shown to be actually in operation, nor
have they been subject to serious process analysis. Interest-
ingly, as we have shown in Chapter 3, Trabasso's work has
demonstrated that children do actually solve transitive inference problems in imaginal rather than logical ways—and
so do adults. Unfortunately there is the possibility, already
noted, that Trabasso's findings could be an artefact of his
training procedures.

Studying language as a means of studying structure

Whilst some authors emphasise the problems of cloaking tasks
in language others take the view that the study of language

per se is a useful strategy for detecting the presence or absence of cognitive structures (Ennis, 1978; Harris, 1975; MacNamara *et al.*, 1976; Povey and Hill, 1975). It is claimed that, 'the comprehension of ordinary language is a particularly favourable field in which to explore children's ability to reason' (MacNamara *et al.*, 1976, p. 69). Ennis (1978) suggests that we should ascertain whether children use and comprehend terms like, 'if . . . then', 'either . . . or' 'implies' and so on.

There are several reasons why this activity is unlikely to be useful in identifying the earliest manifestations of underlying competence. We have already observed that the theory holds that cognitive structures develop before related linguistic structures. Hence, from the point of view of the theory studies of language could have built-in false negative errors. In this respect it is interesting to note that Povey and Hill (1975) claim to have demonstrated a capacity for logical inclusion in five-year-olds and Harris (1975) a capacity for logical inference in five- to six-year-olds. If these results can be sustained and are recognised as subject to false negative errors then these capacities must be assumed to be available even earlier than the authors claim. We are thus left with the problem as to quite when these operations become available.

Additionally, Piaget himself has noted several deficiencies in the use of studies of natural language in the search for cognitive structure (Inhelder and Piaget, 1958). He observes that language expresses thought only in a very rough way and that there are large differences in verbal expression between individuals which are independent of cognitive structure. He concluded that, 'it is fruitless to look for an exclusively verbal or linguistic criterion . . .' (1958, p. 279) and suggested that an analysis of all the actions, statements and proofs of the individual is necessary for the proper identification of his cognitive competence.

These cautions notwithstanding, Inhelder and Piaget seem ready to use linguistic criteria alone in the identification of the formal operational status of subjects (see Inhelder and Piaget, 1958, for example).

MacNamara *et al.* (1976) distinguish between language use and language comprehension. They presented four-year-old children with stories followed by questions. Each story contained a key sentence which in turn contained a key word— pretend, forget or know. The questions tested whether the children had picked up the implications and presuppositions of the key sentence. The responses of the four-year-olds were consistent with the view that they were able to grasp the unstated presuppositions and implications. Unfortunately there is no way of knowing, in this type of study if the children actually solved the problems using deductive reasoning and hence it is impossible to comment on the cognitive competence of these four-year-olds in Piagetian terms.

Similar criticisms may be made of Povey and Hill (1975) (see p. 109 for a description of this study). They showed that five-year-old children exhibited an understanding of the inclusion of sub-classes within classes when questioned about language concepts involving food and people and Piaget suggests that this capacity does not appear until the age of seven or eight (Piaget, 1962). However, Piaget demands that the comprehension of this inclusion must rest on logical necessity and not merely on the memory of figurative knowledge. Povey and Hill did not require this criterion and were hence testing figurative memory rather than operative comprehension.

Clearly such studies can contribute little to the identification and comprehension of a child's cognitive structure until adequate criteria for the identification of language-thought correspondences have been developed. The expression 'if . . . then . . .' could represent a description of an event, a general conditional statement about concrete events derived from particular instances or an abstract hypothesis. Its cognitive status must be determined by applying additional criteria. To be pertinent to the testing of Piaget's theory these criteria must be developed from the theory.

On the whole the above considerations apply to the problems of identifying the earliest manifestations of competences with a view to testing the theory's claims about structure and sequence. We have shown that much of this endeavour remains unproductive because of a lack of uniform criteria for making decisions about manifestations of competence. Where criteria are offered by the Genevans they seem to be inconsistent with the theory and to bias the rejection or acceptance of hypotheses in favour of the theory. Other studies using more justifiable criteria (in terms of Piaget's theory) produce data in conflict with the theory or data which is difficult to evaluate in terms of the theory. This latter is usually attributable to a lack of attention in generating task designs pertinent to Piaget's theory.

Other problems in diagnosing cognitive competence

Quite apart from ascertaining the data of emergence of competencies, the question of the nature of competence has to be explored. In what manner are cognitive structures stored? How are they transformed? How are they interrelated? Problems implicit in previous discussions become more evident in this content.

It is clear in the studies mentioned above that a great deal of the research generated by Piaget's theory involves the *ad hoc* design of tasks, hints, task modifications and questions. Most of these are less 'theory-driven' than 'phenomena-driven'; the modifications are designed to chase or follow up various *post hoc* accounts of the outcomes of experiments. Under these circumstances it is easy to generate data which are open to the charge of lacking generality or even of being artefactual, i.e. arising out of the particular constraints of a particular study. It has already been said, for example, that Trabasso's discovery that subjects build and use imaginal representations to solve transitive inference problems has no generality. Subjects might build such pictures—but only under the conditions of serial presentation of relationships used by Trabasso. Is this what subjects normally do; or can do at best? How is it that they give logical reasons to justify their responses? When does this type of justification develop?

Given the present state of research and its current trends these questions are likely to remain unanswered from Piagetian studies. In part this is because they usually test children over a very narrow range of intellectual processes—frequently only one or two Piagetian operations for example. More importantly, it is because most studies seem to be designed to follow up particular methodological debates. There may be all sorts of reasons for this unhappy state. It seems plausible that one cogent reason is that the theory at the root of this research, i.e. Piaget's theory, is opaque in generating researchable hypotheses which contribute to an accumulation of understanding as opposed to an accumulation of indigestible data.

Any chance of answering questions about the intellectual structure underlying normal functioning must rest on a far broader testing programme in which tasks commonly executed in normal mental functioning are subject to analysis in terms of the theory before being presented to subjects. Responses as functions of task structure could then be more meaningfully analysed in terms of the theory.

A more fundamental problem in the exploration of the nature of structure has been recorded by Smedslund (1977). In order to ascertain whether a child has a particular logical structure or not, one has to assume that he has understood all the task instructions. Alternatively, to decide whether a child has understood a set of instructions we have to take for granted logicality with respect to his received implications. There is thus a circular relationship between logicality and understanding and the researcher must choose which one to study and which to take for granted. It is Smedslund's view that,

> In so far as Piagetian psychologists focus on logicality as a variable . . . they are making an epistemological error . . . children who failed on tasks were often simply described as non-logical and . . . the problem of criteria of understanding has received relatively scant attention in Piagetian literature (1977, p. 4).

Chapter 5

Learning and the development of cognition

In his recent major theoretical work Piaget has emphasised that the main aim of a theory of development is to account for how structures appear and evolve (Piaget, 1970b, 1970c, 1971a, 1972a, 1978). Throughout these texts he presents a continuous and sustained attack on the limitations of empiricism and rationalism as accounts of the origins of structures. Structures are not the products of 'mere' experience, nor are they preformed. 'The problem we must solve, in order to explain cognitive development, is that of *invention* and not mere copying' (Piaget, 1970b, p. 714, his emphasis).

In Piaget's view the child is not born with the logico-mathematical structures at his disposal, nor does he discover them ready made. Rather there is 'an alternative that falls between preformation of logical structure on the one hand and their free or contingent invention on the other' (Piaget, 1971a, p. 67). Whilst experience and social factors certainly play a role in cognitive development, they are insufficient to account for this development. Experience, in Piaget's view, is always filtered through the processes of the subject's actions which in terms of adaptation, 'implies an autoregulation of these actions' (Piaget, 1970b, p. 724). Equally, social transmission cannot alone account for the development of cognitive structures since it begs the questions of how the child understands these transmissions and how the social group got the structures in the first place. Piaget suggests that in addition to the above factors an overriding organising process is needed for two reasons,

The first is that these . . . heterogeneous factors cannot explain a sequential development if they are not in some

139

relation of mutual equilibrium, and that therefore there must exist a[n] organising factor to coordinate them in a consistent, noncontradictory totality. The second reason is that any biological development is, as we know, self-regulatory and that self-regulation processes are even more common at the level of behaviour and the constitution of the cognitive functions (Piaget, 1970b, p. 722).

To maintain this organisation and self-regulation and to account for the construction of structures, Piaget posits a dynamic process called equilibration.

Thus it seems highly probable that the construction of structures is mainly the work of equilibration, defined not by balance between opposite forces but by self regulation; that is equilibration is a set of active reactions of the subject to external disturbances, which can be effective, or anticipated, to varying degrees (Piaget, 1970b, pp. 724, 725).

The equilibration model

The developmental process, as we have described, is seen as a succession of related stages. Each stage is made up of cognitive behaviours which are qualitatively different from those of any other stage. This difference may be described by means of the logical structures which are thought to underlie the stages.

Progress within a stage is manifest by increases in the flexibility and mobility of operations to deal with ever more diverse experiences. Experiences which cannot be dealt with by the operations of the current structure may give rise to disequilibrium.

The equilibrium state which may exist at any point in time is limited in its capacity, and will be prone to dissolution as critical new experiences appear. Thus the equilibrium state which enables the pre-operational child to conceive that a lower level of liquid denotes less liquid, will subsequently suffer perturbations as the child starts to decentre from the height variable to the width variable. Eventual restructuring will produce a new and different equilibrium state which can assimilate more than one variable at a time (see p. 45). The description of the four stages thought to be involved in the equilibration sequence for conservation of quantity raises an important issue. Why should a child progress along such an orderly path, and why *this* orderly path in particular? Piaget (1957b) offers the following probabilistic explanation. In the first place it is most likely that the child will react initially to a single, obvious attribute of the task materials. The argument suggests that in a task in which two dimensions vary, there is a higher probability that one will be seen than that they will both be seen together.

Having now started the equilibration process in this way, probability suggests that it will develop accordingly. Thus, having centred upon one dimension, and produced a response, the child will experience dissatisfaction, particularly when the response is evoked in situations where there is extreme contrast between the dimensions (e.g. when liquid is poured from a tall, thin jar into an extremely wide, shallow one). Under these circumstances there is, it is argued, a high probability that the child may decentre on to the second attribute.

After having centred first on one attribute and then on the other, there is a high probability that they may be employed alternately, perhaps selected on the basis of the degree of contrast in a particular task. Frequent, and perhaps rapid alternation leads to a probability that eventually the third stage will be reached in which both attributes are compared for a certain task.

When the conjunction of two attributes has been elicited several times, comparison across tasks will enable the child to form a logical judgment which will be resistant to novel transformations of the task materials.

> since these displacements of the system are activities of the subject, and since each of these activities consists of correcting the one immediately preceding it, equilibrium becomes a sequence of self regulations whose retroactive processes finally result in reversibility. The latter then goes beyond simple probability to attain logical necessity (Piaget, 1970b, p. 725).

The explanatory value of the equilibration model is said to derive from its being founded on a process with increasing sequential probabilities. Each of the four stages in the above account, 'becomes more probable not *a priori*, but as a function of the present situation, or of the one immediately preceding it' (Piaget, 1970b, p. 725). The explanatory value of this concept has, however, proved very difficult to test. The major effort in appraising the Piagetian transition mechanism has made use of training studies. These studies typically involve the assessment of short-term learning interventions. The method is used by Piagetians and their critics alike. But since the Piagetians do not see learning as a transition process, the use of learning studies to explore transition seems, at first sight, to be paradoxical. It is necessary to say something about the Piagetian notion of learning in order, subsequently, to make sense of training studies.

The role of learning in development

In strictly Piagetian terms learning is very much subordinate to development. The effects of any particular experience are dominated by the subjects' level of cognitive development. Limited effects are expected of learning under external reinforcement which, 'produces either very little change in logical thinking or a striking momentary change with no real comprehension' (Piaget, 1970b, p. 714). In this type of learning Piaget includes the reception of verbal instruction or the observation of the results of transformations about which the subject has made deductions. Learning may be implicated in the generalisation of schemes but very little else is expected of it.

> It is obvious that a stimulus can elicit a response only if the organism is first sensitised to this stimulus. . . . When we say an organism or a subject is sensitised to a stimulus and able to make a response to it, we imply it already possesses a scheme or a structure to which this stimulus is assimilated. . . . This scheme consists precisely of a capacity to respond (Piaget, 1970b, p. 707).

Only when critical matches of experience with cognitive structure are made does a learning experience contribute to cognitive reconstruction.

Essentially . . . learning is subordinate to the subject's level of development. If they are close to the operational level . . . the comparisons they make during the experiment are enough to lead them to compensations . . . but the farther they are from the possibility of operational quantification, the less they are likely to use the learning sequence to arrive at a concept . . . (Piaget, 1970b, p. 716).

Thus it is not always the case that a newly experienced fact will either be assimilated into an existing system or will cause disturbances. It may be that in the example we have used a pre-operational child would not perceive the second attribute of the water containers; but it does not follow that, if it was pointed out to him, he would immediately begin transition through the stages we have described. Piaget (1978) identifies three possible types of response:

- Type a — a new fact may be added without disturbance to the existing system (such as an additional object in a classification prepared to receive it); or, if it contradicts an existing part of the structure it may cause a disturbance. In the latter eventuality the child, though perceiving the disturbing fact, will distort it in order to incorporate it, or may ignore it.
- Type β — the new fact may be integrated into the system by accommodation in the characteristic way we have already described.
- Type γ — in a logico-mathematical situation and in certain causal relationships a superior form of behaviour consists of anticipation of possible variations, and transformation of the system in order to render it compatible with these new possibilities. That is, the formal operation is capable of producing the equivalent of a type β action by the hypothetical generation of potentially disturbing facts.

So the theory asserts that

(i) there exist states of cognitive equilibrium and disequilibrium,

(ii) that an inherent, self regulating feature of cognition is the mechanism which maintains or re-establishes equilibrium in the face of perturbations and

(iii) that some states of equilibrium are 'better' than others.

Piaget (1978) identifies two important categories of disturbance to equilibrium. First there are 'those which are opposed to accommodations' (e.g. due to the resistance of certain objects) and second, 'gaps which leave requirements unfulfilled and are expressed by the insufficiency of a scheme' (Piaget, 1978, p. 18). Clearly it is not possible to predict disturbances solely on the basis of task characteristics. It is necessary to take into account the likely interaction of the logical structure of the task, the likelihood of some specific task presenting resistance and the existing cognitive structures of the child.

Bearing these points in mind it is obviously a very complex undertaking to design short-term learning interventions (i.e. training studies) to explore Piagetian transition mechanisms.

The use of training studies to explore transition

In the Genevan view suitably designed training studies allow the 'observation of cognitive construction under conditions that . . . provide the child with optimal possibilities of interaction with the environment' (Inhelder *et al.*, 1974, p. 10). The object of Genevan training studies is to illuminate the processes of transition in cognitive growth. Such a goal places constraints on the design of the studies and these constraints or design specifications can be derived from the theory. Thus 'Cognitive development results essentially from an *interaction* between the subject and his environment. In terms of successful training procedures, this means that the more active a subject is, the more successful his learning is likely to be' (Inhelder *et al.*, 1974, p. 25). Additionally,

> This idea that schemes, or preconcepts should be co-ordinated and integrated to new structures links up with another point, which is that of the existence of *necessary stages* of development. This hypothesis implies the existence of certain major paths leading to the acquisition of knowledge. Training procedures should steer the subject in the right direction . . . (Inhelder *et al.*, 1974, p. 25).

And finally, whilst the acceleration of cognitive development is possible this 'could only occur if the training procedures in some way resembled the kind of situation in which progress takes place outside an experimental set-up' (Inhelder *et al.*, 1974, p. 24).

In summary the ideal training study would present the subject with experiences which optimally mapped onto his current mental structures at a point where the subject recognised restructuring to be necessary; the experiences would demand action from the subject and the requisite action would be located in the general and spontaneous trend of intellectual growth.

To establish that development has actually taken place in such studies a set of criteria is necessary for judging the outcomes of the interventions. The Piagetians have described their criteria in a number of texts (Inhelder *et al.*, 1974; Piaget, 1970b, for example). To bear witness to cognitive growth the subject's post training behaviour must show 'real comprehension' and 'complete understanding'. The acquisition of elements of figurative knowledge is unimpressive in this context; operative understanding is demanded. These general criteria are operationalised in any specific study by the design of post tests which should show

(i) that new acquisitions are manifest by the deployment of developmentally more mature judgments supported by appropriate explanations,

(ii) that these judgments should be durable,

(iii) that acquired operations should generalise to materials not used in the training study,

(iv) that operations implicit in the trained operation are available, and

(v) that newly acquired operations be resistant to experimental extinction (Inhelder *et al.*, 1974).

This set of criteria raises a number of empirical and theoretical problems. We have discussed some of them in Chapter 4. For example the Genevans continue to insist on judgments plus explanations because the explanation carries the sense of the operationality they seek to assess in a more clear and direct way than a judgment alone. Their view is that judgment only procedures have yet to be designed which at once are unambiguous in interpretation and sufficiently demanding to represent genuine manifestations of Piagetian operations (see Chapter 4 for a discussion of this problem).

The demand for durability of acquired operations seems reasonable. Operations are not seen as figurative images in memory which can fade over time. One of their central properties is that they are enduring. But the problem of timing a post-test is critical. If the post-test is close to training it cannot establish durability. If it is far removed from the training then natural processes of development add to the effects of training and confuse the interpretation of post-test results.

The requirement that operations should generalise to related materials and related operations rests on two other important properties; that is, operations are said to be mobile and to belong to a *structure d'ensemble*. However, quite how much generalisation and interrelationship we can expect is difficult to know. We have indicated that a great number of studies have shown so much asynchrony in the development of particular stages that it would be difficult to define a reasonable expectation in respect of these criteria. Since the theory merely labels this asynchrony as *horizontal décalage* and gives no account of it, these expectations cannot be generated from theory.

With respect to durability and generalisation of acquired operations then, the only sensible source of criteria would come from detailed longitudinal studies which explored the durability and generalisation of operations as they occurred naturally. At present we do not have such studies.

Problems related to testing the relationship of acquired operations to implicit operations, and of assessing resistance to extinction are discussed in the following pages.

It is clear that the criterion problem is a serious one in assessing the outcomes of training studies. Piagetians frequently dismiss the findings of their opponents' training studies on the grounds that they have not demonstrated the growth of 'true comprehension' because they have not operated a full battery of criteria. In this respect it has been noticed by Brainerd (1978) that the Genevans themselves are not averse to using a very limited range of post-testing. On this basis Brainerd dismisses the criterion debate as 'something of a straw man' (1978, p. 78). Our view, however, is that the debate raises matters of considerable significance which demand resolution.

It must be emphasised that the Genevans intend training studies to contribute to an understanding of the transition mechanisms in cognitive growth; they are not interested merely in establishing that interventions can produce change. Rather, they seek to explore the quality of that change. Their specification for a training study clearly takes the grand theory and the equilibration model for granted and their research in this respect is intended to look at the 'fine print' of developmental mechanisms.

The results of training studies

In the following sections we endeavour to avoid two pitfalls. First it is not our intention to review the massive number of training studies in print. Many have addressed themselves to the 'How much can be learned and how soon' question and have, in our view, contributed little to an understanding of anything. Equally limited in their theoretical contribution to understanding cognitive development is that class of training studies which have explored the correlates of cognitive acquisitions. The relationships between training and IQ, training and social class, and training and other diffuse variables have little to say about Piaget's theory. General collections, reviews and commentaries are available elsewhere (Brainerd and Allen, 1971; Glaser and Resnick, 1972; Kuhn, 1974; Modgil and Modgil, 1976; Strauss, 1972).

The second pitfall we wish to avoid is that of taking Piaget's theory for granted and hence too readily receiving the results of Genevan intervention studies. Our intention is to use the Piagetian specification for training studies to identify those claims and assumptions which are generated from the theory and are expressly thought to have empirical mileage in the comprehension of growth mechanisms. We then use appropriate training studies to examine and evaluate these claims.

Examination of the Genevan specification for a training study which we outlined above, reveals the following claims and assumptions.

1 That a natural sequence of acquisition is an optimal sequence.
2 That learning processes in which the subject is active are better than processes in which the subject is not active.

3 That there are special paths or necessary sequences to learning.
4 That trained attainments are different from natural attainments.
5 That subjects cannot profit from learning if they do not already possess appropriate structures.

1 *Is a natural sequence optimal?*

It is Inhelder's claim that intervention would bring about development but this 'could only occur if the training procedures in some way resembled the kind of situation in which progress takes place outside an experimental set-up' (Inhelder *et al.*, 1974, p. 24). It is not clear what claim is being made here. It could be a form of the 'Mother Nature knows best' argument and has recently been taken as such by Brainerd (1978). In his view, the accolade paid to spontaneous development as 'best' development is a contemporary vestige of the influence of Rousseau. If this is the basis of the claim then serious criticism may be brought to bear on it. In Chapter 3 our excursion into cross-cultural studies showed that, in Piagetian terms at least, Mother Nature has been singularly remiss in not providing for the spontaneous development of concrete and formal operations. In this case we are left with no analogue in spontaneity on which to base a training study. However, it is our view that Brainerd is quite wrong to implicate the spirit of Rousseau in this claim. Rousseau's philosophy was a revolt against the intellectual systems of the Age of Reason and a cry for the spontaneous expression of *la sensibilité*. It seems unlikely that such a philosophy would be used to prop up the development of systems of logical operations.

In our, possibly charitable, view the claim here is one for validity rather than a value statement about human nature. There are processes of spontaneous development. If we wish to study these processes then valid interventions must be located in what we understand of those processes. Other interventions are studying something else. Whilst this interpretation of the claim might make it easier for empirical workers to stomach, it does not make it much easier to work with, since it assumes that we actually know something about developmental processes, 'outside an experimental set-up'. In fact we know little, if anything at all, about this. To take this claim seriously demands either that we abandon the design of interventions until massive programmes of ecological observation have taken place or that we take Piaget's view for granted.

2 *Learning involving action is better than learning not involving action*

This claim arises directly from the constructivist nature of Piaget's theory. Structures evolve by means of internal mental reorganisations on the part of the subject. These mental reorganisations regulate disturbances brought about as the subject interacts with his environment. 'In terms of successful training procedures, this means that the more active a subject is, the more successful his learning is likely to be' (Inhelder *et al.*, 1974, p. 25). Unfortunately, the claim is essentially untestable because by 'action' the Genevans have in mind not only overt motor acts but also internal mental acts. Inhelder *et al.* go on to observe that 'being cognitively active does not mean that the child merely manipulates a given type of material; he can be mentally active without physical manipulation, just as he can be mentally passive while actually manipulating objects' (1974, p. 25). Since there is no direct way of observing mental activity it is impossible to know which particular training procedures are implicated in such action and which are not. Thus in a *post hoc* fashion it will always be possible to claim that successful training outcomes must, by definition, have demanded mental action whilst negative outcomes cannot have done so. However, Piaget has labelled some procedures which are particularly unlikely to produce cognitive development and others which are likely to be more propitious. He has singled out learning under external reinforcement and direct verbal instruction as being likely to produce either 'very little change in logical thinking or a striking momentary change with no real comprehension' (1970b, p. 714). On the other hand, self-discovery on the part of the child is more beneficial in fostering cognitive growth: 'each time one teaches a child something he could have discovered for himself, that child is kept from inventing it and consequently from understanding it completely' (1970b, p. 715).

These claims seem reasonable in terms of the theory. They are based not only on the notion of action but also on the notion of subjective match, i.e. that the subject himself must recognise the match or mismatch between his current structures and ongoing experience. 'Intellectual activity is stimulated if the opportunities for acting on objects, or observing other peoples' actions or for discussions correspond to the subject's level of development' (Inhelder *et al.*, 1974, p. 25). All these are more likely of course if the subject is an active participant in a conversation rather than a passive recipient of instruction.

The Piagetians quote empirical support in favour of their predictions regarding the effects of these training methods. In particular they rely on the work of Smedslund (1961a,b). In these studies Smedslund used direct reinforcement of weight judgments, reinforcement of the addition-subtraction rule and reinforcement of the size-weight rule to train first grade children in the conservation of weight. The subjects comprehensively failed to acquire conservation under these circumstances. It is not entirely clear, however, that Smedslund's conclusions can be used to justify Piaget's comments on the limitations of such 'tutorial' methods. For one thing there are limitations in Smedslund's studies. He used a pan balance on which to demonstrate all the outcomes of transformations. If his subjects did not understand the principle of the balance (and at six years of age this is a distinct possibility), then most of the 'tuition' would be meaningless to them. Additionally there is some confusion regarding the reinforcement of the addition-subtraction rule. The subjects were not allowed to weigh the balls of clay before the addition or subtraction of bits of clay and therefore they could not know whether the balls were equal to begin with. Thus the effect of adding or subtracting bits of clay was not unambiguous. Second, even if Smedslund's study was beyond reproach it would not permit the once and for all conclusion that such tutorial methods are necessarily limited in their effects. Many recent training studies have been quite successful using similar methods.

Gelman (1969) successfully used direct reinforcement to induce number and length conservation. She presented children with three stimuli, two showing the same number or length and one which was different. The child selected the stimuli which were the same and was given a token for correct choices. Conservation judgments improved dramatically.

Explanations, which were not reinforced, also improved, the training transferred to conservation of quantity and the improvements were evident two weeks later.

Other tutorial methods including simple correction (in which pre-tests are re-administered several times with feedback and/or reinforcement); rule learning (in which specific rules thought to be implicated in conservation are demonstrated or stated); and observation learning (in which children who fail a conservation test see a live or film model successfully taking the same test) have shown large learning effects which meet the usual Genevan criteria. (For reviews see Brainerd, 1973b, 1977b; and Zimmerman and Rosenthal, 1974.)

A key question is whether these tutorial methods work as well as discovery methods. No convincing, direct comparisons seem available. Thus we are left to draw contrasts across different studies using different samples of children and different materials. Inhelder *et al.* (1974) have collected together a number of Genevan training studies which use methods involving discovery processes. Over the six studies presented an average of 32 per cent of the children made no progress at all—these children typically being the ones judged to be non-conservers on the pre-tests. Studies using tutorial methods generally manage to bring about more impressive results than this. For example, Sheppard (1974) used demonstrations and reinforcement techniques to train conservation of quantity. All his subjects were non-conservers and yet more than 30 per cent achieved conservation whilst all of the rest made some progress. Sheppard's subjects generalised their acquisition to untrained concepts and sustained their gains over a two month interval.

Thus it seems that tutorial methods criticised by Piaget work well in inducing cognitive gains to meet Piagetian criteria. Where it is possible to compare them with the favoured activity/discovery methods the tutorial procedures seem superior. The data presented cast doubt on Piaget's claim. What follows from this? These studies say little about the equilibration model. It could be that the model of the pre-operational child is wrong. If we could accord him more elaborate intellectual processes than the Genevans seem prepared to, then it would not be unreasonable to expect him to make sense of the instruction typically given in these studies.

It could be that the criteria for judging acquisitions are not sufficiently stringent—albeit the studies quoted used the criteria set down by Piaget and his colleagues. The criterion problem seems a more likely source of the disconfirmation than the description of the pre-operational structures. Training studies typically provide the child with pieces of information, discrete rules or processes or direct his attention to particular dimensions of arrays. However, Piaget sees conservation as demanding a unique coordination of capacities and as a consequence a battery of post-testing techniques represents an uncomfortable specification of this attainment. This is why Piagetians require the child to demonstrate that his judgments are based on explanations manifesting his sense of the logical necessity of a conservation response. We return to this problem later. Suffice to say for the moment that casting doubt on an empirical claim made from the theory does not damage the theory in any clear way. As we shall see however, many defences make the theory untestable.

3 *Are there special paths or necessary sequences to learning?*

This claim arises in part from the equilibration model and in part from the Genevan view of evidence from cross-cultural studies. In Piaget's theory of structures, 'Necessity is the outcome of learning' (1971a, p. 62). Thus outcomes are not pre-ordained but once particular compensating or regulatory processes are set in train particular outcomes become increasingly inevitable, 'Construction, in being constantly regulated by equilibration requirements ... yields a necessity' (1971a, p. 67).

Some of Piaget's colleagues vacillate over the exact meaning of this notion. Inhelder *et al.* (1974) observe that the notion of necessary stages implies 'the existence of certain major paths leading to the acquisition of knowledge. Training procedures should steer the subject in the right direction . . .' (p. 25). However, on the next page they note that, 'Variations are, however, possible and it is certainly not true that for each acquisition there is only one predetermined construction process', whilst on p. 270 they return to the view that, 'leading to the elementary concepts of conservation, there are necessary paths . . . within certain limits, variations in rate and direction of development are possible, but crucial steps cannot be omitted'.

We have shown (in Chapter 3) that Piaget takes the view that cross-cultural research gives empirical support to this conclusion and yet close examination of the evidence suggests that this is a doubtful claim. In particular, data suggest such a degree of asynchrony in the development of related structures that it would be extremely difficult to draw on empirical studies to inform the design of the order in which experiences or operations should be developed. If such an order or sequence is not empirically based, then the appeal to 'lead subjects in the right direction' must be founded on *a priori* reasons. If this is the case, there is no possibility of testing the success or failure of such a training sequence by empirical means. There is no point, for example, in testing the relative merits of training for identity prior to training for conservation (or vice versa) because, by definition, identity precedes conservation. Any finding which contradicted this notion must be put down to measurement error.

4 *Are trained attainments different from natural attainments?*

Conceiving learning as the elaboration of within-stage competence rather than the development of between-stage structural change, Piagetians are suspicious of the nature of trained acquisitions. The panoply of post-tests that subjects of training studies must face is intended to establish that some substantial emergent function has developed rather than a response set or a habit. As part of this armoury of tests Smedslund (1961b) introduced the notion of experimental extinction. Having obtained conservation judgments on the equivalence of weight of two balls of clay, Smedslund secretly removed a piece from one of the balls and demonstrated that they were not the same weight. The question was, how would the subjects account for this? Of 11 trained conservers none of them gave an explanation consistent with their newly acquired belief in conservation. Six out of thirteen natural conservers asserted the logical necessity that 'something must have dropped on the floor'. The trained conservers were said to exhibit 'experimental extinction'. Their trained conservation behaviour was assumed not to rest on any notion of logical necessity but on contingent responses. Since then Piagetians have taken the resistance to experimental extinction as a symptom of a qualitative difference between constructed and instructed conservation.

Another form of testing the same notion is by means of counter-suggestion (Kingsley and Hall, 1967). In this procedure a loaded question is asked: 'Which piece of clay will be heavier?' To which a conservation answer must be that they are the same. Using this method Kingsley and Hall compared the resistance to counter suggestion of natural conservers of weight with subjects who had been trained to conserve weight. All the natural conservers succeeded on every test in the battery except the counter suggestion, on which they all failed. However, three out of seventeen trained conservers succeeded in resisting counter-suggestion.

On the basis of Smedslund's study and that of Kingsley and Hall it is clear that 'resistance to extinction' is not a good indicator of the status of conservation. In a review of nine studies using this criterion (Hall and Kaye, 1978) two major results are clear. Large numbers of natural conservers extinguish, and large numbers of trained conservers do not. Indeed, in an earlier review (Kuhn, 1974) it was recommended that this criterion be dropped because it did not distinguish between different types of conserver.

Thus this criterion used to discriminate between natural and trained conservation may be rejected on psychometric grounds. However, there seem to be more substantial reasons for querying why it was ever used in the first place. Piaget himself uses the expression 'logically necessary' to convey the force of emergent operationality. Results which may be used by trial and error are later seen as possible or probable and subsequently felt to be and known to be logically necessary and, 'this logical "necessity" is recognised not only by some inner feeling, which cannot be proved, but by the intellectual behaviour of the subject who uses the newly mastered deductive instrument with confidence and discipline' (Piaget, 1971b, p. 316). However, Piaget clearly recognises that to organise our dealings with the environment in terms of logical necessity is to dispense with accommodation and under these circumstances our interchanges with the physical world would be maladaptive. Drawing on an analogy with science, Piaget notes, 'If physics proceeds by assimilating reality to logico-mathematical models, then it must increasingly accommodate them to new experimental results. It cannot dispense with accommodation because its models would then remain subjective and arbitrary' (1970b, p. 709). If we present children with evidence contrary to their logico-mathematical models it is not clear why we should expect them to dispense with accommodation and insist on logical necessity. Indeed, in terms of adaptation there is every reason to expect the converse.

These comments do not 'prove' that there is no difference between natural and trained conservers. They do demonstrate that the criterion of logical necessity seems unnecessary and indeed misleading in terms of the theory and untenable in terms of psychometrics. We would not agree with Kuhn (1974) however, in recommending the abandonment of this notion. Indeed further exploration of children's reactions to extinction procedures might prove more useful in assessing fundamental processes than continuing concern about differentiating between natural and trained conservers. Extinction procedures clearly place children in a situation in which they must deal with disconfirming evidence. One interesting result is that younger, natural conservers are more resistant to extinction than older natural conservers (Hall and Kaye, 1978). This might have something to say about the 'protected' status of a new theory as opposed to the malleable status of a later model. We are simply making the point here that in Piagetian terms training studies are conceived as making a contribution to an understanding of growth mechanisms; too frequently this goal is lost in the discussion of technical issues in which the overall strategy is buried under tactical considerations.

5 *Do subjects with appropriate structures profit more from learning than subjects without appropriate structures?*

Piaget predicts that the results of training experiments will 'vary very significantly as a function of the initial cognitive levels of the children' (1970b, p. 715). This prediction is extensively borne out in Genevan training studies. Inhelder *et al.* (1974) demonstrate time and time again that 'frankly pre-operational' children make far less progress and show far less generalisation than transitional children.

In quantitative terms this is neither a profound claim nor an interesting verification. As Brainerd (1978) points out, it amounts to no more than saying that it is easier to teach children who know something about the subject at the outset than it is to teach those who know nothing at the outset.

Additionally, such a claim is not unique to Piaget's theory. Consequently, verification of the prediction supports every learning theory from which it could be generated—that is every learning theory.

However, the claim regarding training-development interactions appears in two other forms. The first is that the level of development can actually limit the effects of training: 'operativity is malleable only within certain limits . . . children at the pre-operational level do not acquire truly operational structures . . .' (Inhelder and Sinclair, 1969, p. 19). The second form is that training-developmental level interactions produce qualitatively different outcomes which are illuminative of the processes of cognitive growth. The collection of studies by Inhelder *et al.* (1974) is an example of an attempt to make progress in this respect. Below we comment on each of the two forms of the Piagetian view regarding treatment-developmental level interactions.

In the light of empirical studies, the view that developmental level constrains the effects of learning appears untenable. There are many studies which show that children who fail all pre-tests of conservation administered can nevertheless learn the concept of conservation in pre-tested areas and transfer their training to untrained areas. Additionally many of these studies have used pre-school children and trained them to conservation competence (see Brainerd, 1977b, 1978 for reviews). Most of these studies satisfy all the Genevan criteria including transfer to untrained areas and durability. Thus if 'true comprehension' is in doubt we must await a clearer specification of what the Piagetians 'truly comprehend' by the notion of conservation. The doubt regarding the claim that developmental level might constrain the effects of learning might be resolved in one of two ways. It could be dissolved in the brew of the criterion problem and hence be made essentially untestable. Conversely it might be necessary to re-write the specification of the pre-operational child's competence. It could be that training is evoking and eliciting competence which is already there. Certainly this possibility is consistent with most of the lines of evidence which we have examined in this and earlier chapters.

The second form of the claim that development constrains learning refers to the possibility that interesting qualitative differences may emerge when such interactions are studied and that these qualitative differences might illuminate our understanding of the processes of growth. Descriptions of these interactions are presented by Inhelder *et al.* (1974). Unfortunately the descriptions of change-between-structures are exceedingly vague and couched in the same language that is used to describe the general model of equilibration which is thus taken for granted.

In the introduction to our treatment of training studies we emphasised that the Piagetians considered such work should illuminate the processes of change rather than explore the quantity of change. In our view training studies have rarely addressed themselves to this problem and we have used their methods and data to comment on more general issues raised by Piaget's stance on learning and its relationship to development.

In terms of research on the process of equilibration the Genevans consider their own work as exploratory and that 'little is as yet known about the mechanisms of transition from one major stage to the next . . .' (Inhelder *et al.*, 1974, p. 14). As we have shown, their specification for training studies takes their own theory for granted and contains a number of embedded assumptions which we feel have doubtful validity. Rather than gather more of the same kind of study it seems more profitable to us, and indeed essential, to locate training studies within a context of more broadly conceived longitudinal studies (which would provide more substantial bases for deciding on criteria of attainment, generalisation, etc., and for designing appropriate intervention schedules), and more narrowly conceived experimental studies, in which clearly articulated hypotheses, preferably drawn from contrasting theories, should be juxtaposed to test alternative interpretations of change mechanisms. There is work of this sort available and we now turn our attention to it to examine some of its limitations and implications.

Experimental studies of the dynamics of cognitive growth

Murray, Ames and Botvin (1977) and Bower (1974) focused on the dynamics of cognitive restructuring rather than on the inputs and outputs of tasks and performances.

Murray and his colleagues employed cognitive dissonance to induce cognitive conflict. The technique involved determining whether a child was a conserver, non-conserver, or transitional, then asking him to give a reason to another child which was contrary to his own reason.

Ninety-six children drawn from the kindergarten and first three grades of schools in New York were given a battery of eight traditional conservation tasks. On this basis they were categorised as non-conservers (score 0), transitionals (scores 5–10), and conservers (score 16). In a second session they were then told to pretend to give alternative conservation responses to another child. Afterwards they were given a post-test of the same eight pre-test items. A control group was also given pre- and post-tests.

Analyses indicated that non-conservers and transitionals made large gains in conservations after the experimental procedure of recounting conserver-explanations (Table 5.1). Those children who were already conservers, on the other hand, showed no tendency to regress; a result predicted by Genevan theory, though not by conventional cognitive dissonance theory.

Table 5.1 Mean scores for conservers, transitionals and non-conservers before and after pretence

Group	Conservers	Transitional		Non-conservers	Control
Pretence	NC	C	NC	C	
Pre-test	16.00	7.45	6.67	0.00	3.70
Post-test	16.00	15.50	10.16	14.50	4.79
P	n.s.	0.001	n.s.	0.001	n.s.

(After Murray *et al.*, 1977.)

The authors concluded that the results were consistent with the notion that cognitive conflict between true belief and pretended belief can motivate cognitive change and development.

A subsequent investigation confirmed the previous findings, and the introduction of new conservation tasks into a post-test seven or eight days after the experiment suggested that the gains made by non-conservers were not temporary and that the operations, like those of the original conservers were resistant to extinction and transferable to other problems.

Whilst these experiments look convincing, there are limitations. It is possible, as the authors admit, that the conservation pretence employed by non-conservers and some transitionals, could have been 'parroted' in the post-tests. The reasons used in the experimental pretence were an identity component and a 'nothing added or subtracted' component, and the latter was used only once in post-test, so the authors concluded that the explanation was unlikely.

A more interesting issue relates to the degree of conflict experienced by the children. Table 5.1 shows that the transitionals who gave conservation pretence subsequently produced near perfect conservation on post-test, and this is what we might expect from Piaget's four stages of equilibration. It is also clear that the initial non-conservers did almost as well however, and whilst an experimental 'ceiling effect' may account for some of this, the results are impressive.

Another 'conflict' study was reported by Bower (1974). To compare a simple learning model with Piaget's 'reconstruction through conflict' model, Bower subjected two groups of 80-day-old infants to training schedules to examine their effects on performance on the Mundy-Castle task. In this task infants track an object as it appears consecutively in each of four portholes in the order, bottom left, top left, top right, bottom right. At twelve weeks infants are usually able to anticipate the appearance of the object but only by simple eye movements such as place-to-place tracking. A little later their tracking begins to show interpolation of the trajectory between portholes.

Bower's two groups initially demonstrated the simple tracking behaviour. One group was then given circular tracking training (identical in operation to the more sophisticated performance on the Mundy-Castle task) whilst the other group was given 'oscillation tracking' training. In terms of the hypothesised 'rules of tracking' of children of this age, 'oscillation' training is rich in conflict. In simple behavioural terms, however, it is no more advanced than the simple tracking behaviour initially deployed on the Mundy-Castle task.

Piaget's theory would predict that the second group would show significantly better performance on the task because of the development arising out of conflict-provoking training.

This prediction was confirmed by Bower; the conflict-trained group exhibited four times as many trajectory interpolations as the first group on post-training tests.

Clearly, from the two studies quoted, conflict is implicated in cognitive advance. Unfortunately experimental studies of this sort can say little more. They leave us ignorant of the mechanisms of conflict.

Longitudinal studies

Kuhn (1974) made a plea that training studies should be embedded in more extensive programmes of longitudinal research. Longitudinal studies, she argued, could supply us with more detailed information about norms of development and normal processes of cognitive growth. On this basis we should be able to define criteria of acquisition more clearly, design more appropriate training schedules and time interventions on a more systematic basis.

As far as we are aware, such detailed and ambitious longitudinal studies are not available. The expense and other resource problems of implementing such studies are well known. Additionally a number of strategic decisions have to be taken in their design which, in Kuhn's specification, would require at the outset most of the knowledge these studies would be intended to collect. Batteries of tests would have to be chosen, suitable criteria adopted, testing programmes preplanned and the like. It is not surprising therefore, that longitudinal studies tend to be required to check out cross-sectional findings rather than to inform cross-sectional interventions.

Typical of this approach is a study reported by Neimark (1975). Children were studied over a four-year period (grades 3–6). Their developmental status was assessed using Piagetian tests, and measures of cognitive style and general problem solving facility were also taken. The only substantial result with regard to Piaget's theory was that, 'detailed examination of the longitudinal data shows individual development to proceed in a stepwise fashion through temporary transitional phases. This longitudinal pattern is in accord with Piagetian theory' (Neimark, 1975, p. 173). Clearly this is a confirmation of Piaget's observations of stage attainment and says nothing at all about the process of development.

Concluding comments

It is clear that little is known about the functional processes at the heart of Piaget's theory of cognitive development. It has proved difficult for research workers to agree on what processes are involved in the manifestations of underlying competence (conservation for example) and consequently much research has been either bogged down in, or joyously preoccupied with, the criterion problem. It has proved even more difficult, indeed impossible, to find reference to manifestations of assimilation and accommodation at transitional points. Indeed these words seem to be defined by the very phenomena they are invoked to explain. Piaget's account of transition seems untestable. Since his account of learning is so circumscribed as to define it out of a role in transition it seems peculiar to find learning studies being used to explore these processes. It is not surprising that such studies have come to nothing in the hands of Genevans and have followed red herrings in the hands of others. Piaget's view of learning seems to require a great deal of special pleading to explain away the results of his critics.

Chapter 6

Retrospect and prospect

In Chapter 1 we described a set of criteria by which scientific theories may be judged. In respect of some of these criteria Piaget's theory is enormously successful. It is parsimonious and wide ranging. With a few central concepts almost the whole range of human cognitive experience is encompassed. The development of specific concepts such as space and time is handled in the same terms as broader issues such as the child's understanding of geometry and ultimately, the child's conception of the world. The theory has raised fascinating questions and continues to do so. The vast flow of Piagetian literature shows no sign of ebbing.

Yet in the previous pages we have accumulated a number of criticisms which imply that all is not well with Piaget's theory. Indeed we feel that this body of criticism clearly suggests that the theory, where testable, proves inadequate. More seriously, it is in many respects untestable. In this sense it acts as a spur to the accumulation of 'literature' but not to the accumulation of understanding.

Fortunately some recent attempts to develop comprehensive theories of cognitive development have moved away from strictly Genevan lines. Since these attempts draw heavily on Piaget's studies they may be seen as genuine products of his theory and in that sense his work has been fertile. In subsequent sections we describe two of these developments but before doing so we summarise the major shortcomings of Piaget's work.

Central criticisms of Piaget's theory

In 1963 Flavell published his classic work on Piaget's theory. In a concluding section he described four major criticisms which could be levelled at the work. There were problems with Piaget's methods and with the treatment of language-thought correspondences. Additionally it was felt that there was an inadequate account of individual differences and of the effects of experience. Finally, Flavell claimed that there was an overelaborate treatment of structure. Sixteen years on, exactly the same kinds of criticism can be made.

Piaget and his colleagues continue to extol the virtues of the clinical method, recently re-named the method of 'critical exploration' (Inhelder *et al.*, 1974). This method, in which the 'experimenter' matches his questions and tasks according to his perceptions of the subject's line of responses, is indeed highly suited to exploration. However, even in principle, it seems a poor foundation on which to rest a theory. It affords no opportunity for eliminating alternative accounts of the subject's difficulties or successful strategies, and we have noted (especially in Chapters 3 and 4) just how many alternative accounts can be made available. In practice the method is even less impressive as a means of securing data. Records of the experimenter's interventions and the subject's responses are necessarily selective. Reports of the studies tend to mix fact with interpretation. (See Karmiloff-Smith and Inhelder, 1975, for example.) Since the major portion of the data collected is in the form of subjects' protocols, reporting is also necessarily selective and genuine replications are almost impossible. Piaget is clearly cognisant of these methodological problems (Piaget, 1929) but chooses to ignore them.

In 1963 it was possible to accuse the Genevans of studying 'nothing but' vocabulary growth. Nowadays critics appreciate that even vocabulary growth is not 'nothing but' vocabulary growth so the criticism is unlikely to be made. And yet much of the sense of the criticism still stands. Piagetian tasks demand an understanding of terminology and justification couched in verbal expressions of complex relationships which often seem far in excess of the elemental notion being tested. This would be perfectly acceptable if some basic conceptual work had been done on giving a theoretical account of language-thought correspondences or at least on classifying them. Instead, the reverse is true; the primacy of cognition over language is asserted. The problem is that we have a theory of cognitive development which gives little attention to language development and yet which relies heavily on verbal behaviour for data. The difficulty is manifest in the criterion problem. Additionally, as Smedslund (1977) has pointed out, in order to study logicality, comprehension is taken for granted. The Genevans have paid no attention to this problem, either at a practical, methodological level or at a conceptual level. We are not suggesting that there is any single, unidirectional relationship between language and thought. It does seem, however, that Piaget and his colleagues continue to be uncritical of their major source of data and their major interpretive procedures.

In Chapter 2 we noted that Piaget uses an epigenetic model of development. The fundamental questions raised by an epigenetic view are:

(a) What properties characterise each stage?
(b) What is the end state (goal) of the entire process?
(c) What processes are involved in transforming one stage into the next?

Answers to these questions would provide the general laws of development. There is little need, in this respect, to consider individual differences or the role of experience and it is no surprise therefore that Piaget gives these issues scant attention. This is not to say that he does not recognise that there are differences between individuals, nor is experience left without a role to play in cognitive development. Indeed, with respect to the latter it is clear that his interactionist theory makes experience necessary to development. Yet it is also clear that the effects of experience are severely circumscribed. Experience properly matched to ongoing structures enables necessary outcomes to be realised. Thus experience provides the energy for development. Differences in experience in terms of both nature and quality of match, account in part for differences in rates of development between individuals. But these differences do not inform our understanding of the fundamental epigenetic questions and hence no serious treatment of them is to be expected.

However, if we take the view that differences between individuals within a stage are as impressive as their stage-defined similarities, or if evidence suggests that experience does not merely produce 'necessary' results but radically alters behavioural potentials then these two concepts demand particular attention. We believe that cross-cultural studies have shown both of these results. Unfortunately, Piaget gives no account of individual differences and his account of the role of learning (viewed in the light of our survey in Chapter 5) seems either untestable or wrong.

Flavell (1963) put forward the view that, 'Piaget has in general attributed too much structure and system to the child's thought' (p. 438). We have cited a catalogue of evidence showing heterogeneity of behaviour where a structural account might predict homogeneity. Piaget's structural account does not appear to predict actual behaviours. To justify this mismatch a distinction has been made between competence and performance and Piaget's theory has been taken to be a description of competence. This distinction however poses serious empirical problems. Is competence equated with the earliest emergence of a function? Suppose it is. We cannot make predictions about a child's behaviour on this basis since the manifestation of this competence is contingent upon a variety of extra-structural factors. To predict the child's behaviour we would need to grade all relevant tasks in terms of their capacity to evoke pertinent structures at various stages of development. But Piaget's theory tells us almost nothing about task characteristics.

In addressing this problem in the formal operational stage, where Piaget's own data seemed inadequate for the structures proposed, Flavell concluded that, 'the time simply may not be ripe . . . for models of such apparent rigor and such real constraints and rigidities . . .' (pp. 439-40). We have since seen Piaget (1972a) acknowledge the extent of environmental factors and modify the claim to a 'stage' of formal operations.

Given these serious problems with the notion of structure we cast a critical eye on the structuralist's notion of 'stage'. Flavell raised the question, 'can the construct "stage" really serve any theoretical purpose other than to mislead us . . . ?' (p. 442). In 1963 Flavell concluded that the notion of stage was a useful means of describing development from a *process* point of view rather than a *person* point of view. The notion would evidently enable us to explore questions such as (i) do task and individual variables affect the number, nature and sequence of stages, (ii) if so, is this variation associated with process variables and (iii) what are the effects of various training methods?

Sixteen years after Flavell we feel the data we have examined support the following contentions:

(i) It is difficult to test Piaget's notion of 'stage' since the sequence described seems to be no more than definitional. Second, it is a notion protected by safety clauses such as 'task resistance' and *horizontal décalage* such that any potentially conflicting data can be explained away.

(ii) The notion of 'stage' creates more conceptual problems than it solves. Furthermore, contemporary process research (e.g. Trabasso, 1977) proceeds perfectly well without the concept of stage and evidence of emergent functions in this research is singularly lacking.

(iii) Flavell's questions can be researched without the notion of stage (except of course where the wording takes the notion for granted). The notion of 'stage' seems, quite simply, unnecessary.

In addition to Flavell's four points we feel there is a fifth, more serious criticism to be made of the theory. In our view Piaget offers no adequate *explanation* of cognitive development. Having adopted an epigenetic model of development Piaget is committed to offering some account of how structures evolve from stage to stage. In epigenetic terms, an explanation of development would involve, at a first level, a detailed description of stage structure. At a second level, explanation would take the form of predictions of structural change. A stronger form of explanation involves describing the elemental mechanisms which bring that change about. We saw in Chapter 4 that Piaget's descriptions of stage structure were in many important respects inadequate. In Chapter 5 we concluded that his predictions of structural change consequent upon training were inaccurate. It is hardly surprising then that his account of the mechanism of change leaves something to be desired. The notion of equilibration as a self-regulating mechanism at the heart of the cognitive construction process is essentially a concept deriving from the basic philosophy of the theory. Early critics viewed the concept with suspicion in terms of the contribution it might make to empirical work (Bruner, 1959; Flavell, 1962). The idea is typically defined by pointing to examples (Inhelder,

1972; Inhelder *et al.*, 1974; Piaget, 1970b). As far as we know, no progress has been made in exploring the adequacy of this notion as an explanatory concept. Thus our most serious criticism is that Piaget offers no explanation of cognitive development other than in terms of the philosophical conviction that it is necessary to adopt a constructivist model, a necessity which arises out of his demolition of rationalism and empiricism.

The empirical value of Piaget's concepts of structure and transition is exceedingly vague. Thus it is difficult to predict actual performance on tasks which apparently demand the same logical processes but differ in some stimulus feature. The following 'non-logic' features have been shown to affect performance radically; the presence of redundant features (Hamel, 1974); differences in the perceptual salience of critical features (Odom, 1978); and the information load of a problem (e.g. the capacity to adopt a systematic strategy in writing out multiple combinations varies as the number of dimensions to be combined, Scardamalia, 1977). To develop an understanding of actual performances on task it is clear that an analysis of the 'objective' task structure is insufficient. We need to determine how the task is subjectively encoded before we can write out problem-performance links. It is not helpful to define the notion of 'stage' in terms of a set of operations if these operations are themselves operationalised in terms of a set of tasks which is far from homogeneous in its demands in respect of the critical features we have listed above. And if the notion of stage is made diffuse in this sense, then the notion of transition between stages is necessarily vague. If we are not clear about what is going through transition, accounts of transition must be hazy.

Recently attempts have been made to develop models of performance which account for some of the problems we have discussed above. Typically these theoretical developments involve some combination of Piaget's theory with information processing theory. In what follows we discuss two such developments.

Information processing accounts of cognitive development

Information processing theory attempts to provide a step-by-step account of cognitive acts as opposed to a structural account of cognitive competence.

Adaptation to the environment requires interactions based on adequate representations of the environment. The product of cognitive development, in information processing terms, is the construction of such representations built on previous interchanges. Thus an active role is ascribed to the child and the growth of memory is the key feature of development.

The model of memory used by many contemporary information processing theorists is illustrated in Figure 6.1. The basic model is not without critics. Here we are simply using it for purposes of illustration.

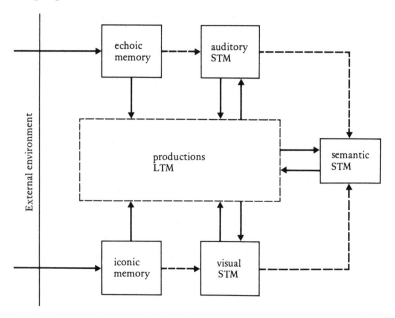

Figure 6.1 *Structure of the memory system (after Klahr and Wallace, 1976)*

Memory is regarded as being made up of a number of stores (Neisser, 1967). The exact properties of these stores is in dispute, but in essence echoic and iconic memory are sensory memories which, for a very short period of time, retain all that falls on the senses of hearing and sight. Material in these sensory stores is subject to very rapid decay—a process dictated by the physiological mechanisms of the ear and eye. Material may, however, be selected and transferred to the auditory or visual short-term memories and subsequently into long-term memory. Particular selections, and the mode of processing, are dominated by psychological strategies but the quantity of material processed in STM is limited by the structural constraints of this process. These structural constraints can be minimised by the development of efficient processing strategies. Memory processes are two-way in action. STM determines to some degree what is selected and processed in echoic memory and hence what can be transferred.

The limitations of the structure of memory conflict with the demand for effective interaction with the environment. Effective interaction demands optimal information processing. There have to be selections of relevant from irrelevant information and of the significant from the trivial for example. It is considered that this is best achieved by 'maximising information throughput' (Klahr and Wallace, 1976). Unfortunately the structural limitations of STM constrain this. STM can process only a small number of 'pieces of information' at any one moment. On the other hand, what counts as a piece of information can become increasingly elaborate as methods of coding develop. (Thus a piece of information can be a single digit in a telephone number or the sense of a whole theory carried in a formula such as $E = mc^2$.) It is the elaboration of coding procedures which is at the heart of cognitive development.

The development of information processing

In information processing terms it is thought necessary to postulate certain innate processes for dealing with the earliest interactions with the environment. It is necessary from birth to recognise and code features of the environment and to detect regularities in these features. Thus a set of discrimination processes and a set of pattern recognisers are postulated. Using these processes consistent features of the environment can be detected, redundant information can be ignored, and useful information can be represented in LTM in 'chunks' of ever increasing elaboration. A repertoire of consistent features is built up in LTM. This can then guide LTM so that information in STM can be treated in a more structured form than is possible on the basis of innate discrimination processes. The sequence of pattern recognition leading to input organisation which increases the power of the pattern recognisers continues.

The construction and use of the repertoire of representations is made maximally efficient by a system of procedures which eliminate redundant processes. The redundancy-elimination procedures are also innate. The action of the whole information processing system is well illustrated by an example from Wallace (1978, p. 42).

> In the case of the development of quantification, the innate processes first use the common consistent sequences to predict the effect of transformations on the relationship between the initial and resultant collections. The relationship is simply read off the sequence without carrying out quantification after the transformation. The predictions are verified by quantitative comparison with the initial collection. Success in this predictive phase results in confirmation that quantification of the collection after the transformation and the subsequent quantitative comparison constitute unnecessary processing and may be eliminated.

Production systems

To account for particular problem-solving behaviours of a child the information processing theorist asks what a mechanism would require to exhibit the same behaviour as the child. They write their answers in the form of a computer program which contains statements about the task structure, the system's structure and the child's representational structure, i.e. a model of how the child must represent the problem. This account (or theory) of the child's problem solving behaviour must be sufficiently explicitly stated for the computer program to run. Failure to run indicates a failure in expressing an understanding of the behaviour being modelled.

The programs are called production systems and take the form of ordered 'condition-action' links. Such a device is shown in Figure 6.2.

A set of rules is stored in LTM. Each rule contains a

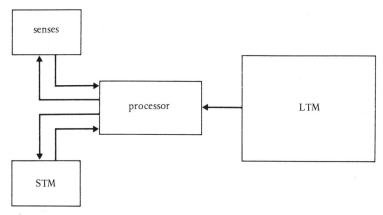

Figure 6.2 *A production system (after Broadbent, 1975)*

specification of the conditions for the rule's use and a specification of the actions of the processor should the rule operate.

The 'condition' side of the condition-action link refers to the contents in STM that represent the system's momentary knowledge state whilst the action side refers to the transformations on STM which include the generation, interruption and satisfaction of goals. Thus the condition-action link contains the ongoing specification of a problem together with an updated display of pertinent information. The system operates to change the symbols in STM or the state of representation of the senses until the problem is 'solved'.

Production system models have been written for representing children's behaviours on class inclusion problems, conservation and transitivity (Klahr and Wallace, 1976). They have been successful in several respects. First the full production system generates correct solutions to such problems. More importantly, other forms can be written which mirror children's failures on these problems and provide insights into the child's limitations. Finally such insights lead to specifications for training studies which have been shown to be effective in bringing about improved performances (Broadbent, 1975).

What are the advantages of such models over Piaget's theory? Some of the obvious advantages are contained in the previous paragraph. The models are specific and testable. From them we can generate predictions with empirical implications. Additionally the general model is more explicit about what is innate. The specified discriminating, pattern-recognising and redundancy-generating mechanisms can be shown to account for the acquisition of a functional LTM repertoire. The process-structure distinction made by Piaget is not required in this model. 'Piaget's structures are replaced by production systems, while the functions of equilibration are discharged by the generally applicable productions . . .' (Klahr and Wallace, 1976, p. 189). There is fundamental similarity between the production system account and Piaget's theory which 'lies in the acceptance of an innate "functional kernel". Innate productions . . . provide the basis of the system's self modification capability, and thus of cognitive development' (ibid.).

Thus the central advantage of such models resides in their testability via computer processing. One serious disadvantage is that in writing in systematic limitations a number of questions is begged about what the limits of human information processing actually are, and how they may be best conceptualised. For example, the production system runs through its rules in a serial fashion whereas there appears to be evidence that humans have ample capacity for parallel processing together with the additional capacity to choose serial or parallel processing as appropriate (Neisser, 1967).

The work of Pascual-Leone

Another original approach to interpretation of Piagetian theory is that of Pascual-Leone. There are two aspects of his work with which we are particularly concerned in the context of our present critique.

He argues (Pascual-Leone, 1976) that North American training studies which attempt to evoke equilibration differ in an important way from Genevan studies. The specific aspects of the theory which are seen by Piaget's own colleagues to encourage training studies (Inhelder *et al.*, 1974) are the assertions that spontaneous transitions are to be expected if (i) many different specific strategies are taking place in separate situations, (ii) conflict is occurring between schemes which were originally developed separately, and which are subsequently activated simultaneously, and (iii) a certain maturational level of the equilibration mechanism is associated with the general *structure d'ensemble* of the corresponding stage. A crucial element in this prescription is the emphasis upon *spontaneous* transitions.

Pascual-Leone maintains that the American studies have emphasised experimenter intervention in attempts to optimise performance. Genevans, on the other hand, simply expose children to a succession of tasks of varying difficulty but common structure, in order to 'render observable this process of spontaneous cognitive-conflict resolution' (1976, p. 272). The apparent conflict between researchers, he suggests, may be resolved by invoking the idea of performance categories as functions of underlying competence which are dependent upon context for their manifestation. Americans and Genevans employ procedures with marked contextual differences.

By introducing the concept of 'learning loops' Pascual-Leone attempts to elaborate the Genevan procedures. 'Learning loops' come into operation in the spontaneous activity which these procedures generate. If a basic sequence of items, a_1, a_2, a_3, is such that they share a common structure, but are graded from most difficult (a_1) to least difficult (a_3), the child may fail on a_1 and a_2 but succeed on a_3. The latter being the easiest, often demands little knowledge and has strong contextual cues. Successive retesting of a_1 and a_2, returning frequently to a_3 as necessary, constitutes the 'learning loop' which 'prompts insights and often leads the subject to discover correct solutions to the hard items' (1976, p. 272).

Whilst loops are themselves ordered from easiest to most difficult, the reverse ordering of items is believed to elucidate the learner's own equilibration process. 'For this reason they are not interested in maximizing learning in ways which may decrease the need for active problem solving' (ibid., p. 275).

In contrast to this approach, studies such as those by Lefebvre and Pinard (1972, 1974) are described as employing an 'executive-learning' method in which external intervention is used to facilitate development. Particularly important in this respect, Pascual-Leone argues, is the fact that these studies force the 'chunking' of task-relevant schemes. This reduces mental processing complexity and thereby renders the task easier.

This explanation may account for some of the conflicting evidence, but in Chapter 5 we described how some training studies produced acquisitions which were stable, and genera-lisable across tasks. Pascual-Leone's analysis does not lead us to anticipate such results by the 'executive-learning' method.

A more dramatic elaboration of the Piagetian position is his attempt to develop a model of the mental processing capacity of the child (Pascual-Leone, 1970). Here he puts for-ward the proposition that stage structure and equilibration may be conceptualised as quantitative constructs involving information storage and processing capacity. Stage, if con-ceived as an abstract structure, offers the possibility of an ordinal scale of intellectual development, the dimension of which would be the informational complexity of a given task as perceived by the individual. A particular stage could then be referred to by the number of 'chunks' of information that could be handled at any one time.

The hypothesis suggests that each individual has the equi-valent of a central computing space, M, which increases systematically during development. A structural stage would be the manifestation of this internal computing system, termed the M operator.

Within the stage, changes could occur if additional infor-mation was learned, although M would remain constant. Furthermore, the maximum capacity of M at any time might be greater than that actually used. He refers to the 'structural M_s' and the 'functional M_f'.

Within the context of a particular task the cues available will have specific degrees of salience; that is, there will be a specific probability that a cue, s, will elicit a response. If the salience is low a higher level of functional M_f operation will be required to deal with it.

With these parameters in mind, the theory develops a model of a repertoire of relatively consistent, 'stage-type' be-havioural units, H, an M operator which transforms or inte-grates subsets of information from H, and a number of laws which organise learning (though the latter are not specified and are not necessary to the explication of H and M).

The structural repertoire, H, is an organised set of reactions which can be translated from one situation to another. With-in it will be schemes which will be inter-related, some super-ordinate to others, and with capacities to elicit or inhibit the evocation of each other. The concept of superordinate and sub-ordinate is analogous to computer programs with subroutines, the author maintains. The concept is also recursive, in that superordinate schemes may themselves be composed of schemes which in turn are superordinate to others. The activation of related schemes requires the action of executive schemes.

The computing space, M, with the schemes of H, provide for the processing of information, and its transformation and coordination into the cognitive system. The maximum number of schemes, or discrete informational elements which can be attended to at one time, that is, the number of channels available in M, is assumed to increase as development progresses.

At the age of five to six years, when verbal mediation is thought by some to make human learning distinct from that of other species (see Chapter 1), the value of the computing space is given as:

$$M = a + 2$$

where a is a constant which operates across all ages. Thus the stage following, that is the earliest form of concrete operations would yield:

$$M = a + 3$$

Several studies are cited by the author in support of this model (Case, 1976; Pascual-Leone, 1970; Parkinson, 1969). In each of these, estimates of the value of M have been found to predict performance on Piagetian tests.

Case, using children from three-and-a-half years to eight-and-a-half years, attempted to train conservation of substance using an apparatus consisting of a specially designed balance scale. When the child guessed correctly which beaker placed upon the scales contained most liquid the scales delivered a marble. Initial training ensured that the children understood the functioning of the balance and were able to equate amount of liquid with weight on the balance.

Four standardised trial procedures were then carried out commencing with a difficult task followed successively by relatively easy and difficult tasks. Thus a 'learning loop' was set up, and no other help or attention-directing ploys were offered. The younger children were given 120 trials and the older ones 60 trials over several weeks. Post-tests of standard Genevan conservation tasks were given immediately and again after five days.

All nine subjects for whom $M = a + 3$ was established by

specific pre-tests, acquired conservation of weight and substance. None of the twelve children with $M = a + 2$, or of those with $M = a + 1$ passed the final post-test. Among controls with equivalent powers of M the conservation of weight was passed by 11 per cent, 0 per cent, and 0 per cent respectively; and the conservation of substance by 33 per cent, 8 per cent, and 0 per cent respectively.

Pascual-Leone interprets the foregoing as evidence that the problem-solving methods incorporating 'learning loops' do not alter the mental complexity of tasks, thus leaving assessment of the organismic developmental factor unchanged. A previous study (Case, 1975) is reported to have shown that the training methods adopted by Lefebvre and Pinard enabled the tasks to be successfully completed by children for whom the M space was defined by $M = a + 2$. That is, they were assumed to have reduced the task requirements.

Whilst this work offers an interesting way of construing Piaget's stage model, and of explaining apparent contradictions in the analyses of empirical studies, the extent to which it provides an advance in our understanding of the process of equilibration is open to doubt.

This approach is much more than an embellishment of Piaget's theory. In our view it presents a fundamentally different approach. If we consider within-stage changes, as seen by Pascual-Leone, we appear to be offered a straightforward behaviourist explanation. That is, the level of performance in a given stage is a direct product of the quantity of information which has been processed. It is true that one may still invoke Genevan notions of assimilation and accommodation, but the interpretation has nothing to say about them.

The translation of stage incompetence into M space limitation is equally fundamental. The young child is not denied certain higher order mental processes or operations. So long as the number of schemes involved in processing a particular operation does not exceed the child's developmentally determined M space limitation then there is no structural reason to deny the possibility or likelihood that the child will possess that operation. A scheme, in Pascual-Leone's view, would only be precluded from a child's repertoire if formal analysis of the acquisition of that scheme showed that acquisition demanded an M space beyond the child's limitations. Case (1974) predicted that it is entirely possible to teach a 'control of variables' scheme to seven- to eight-year-olds since analysis of its acquisition shows it to be within their typical M space range. This prediction was confirmed. The distinction between a functional M space and a structural M space is also important and interesting. There are individual differences in the degree to which M space is used and Pascual-Leone considers the dimension of field dependence-field independence to be implicated in this. Field independent subjects are said to use their M space to capacity $(M_f = M_s)$ whereas field dependents do not $(M_f < M_s)$. It is possible on this basis to predict differential effects of instruction for subjects of different cognitive style, and such predictions have been supported in studies by Case (1972, 1974). Additionally, Neimark's (1975) longitudinal study of the development of formal operational thinking showed that field independent children were more advanced in Piagetian terms than those who were field dependent.

Thus Pascual-Leone's theory offers a maturational component (the development of M space), an information processing orientation to task analysis and behavioural productions, a dimension for handling an important aspect of individual differences, and an account of scheme acquisition which, whilst apparently behaviourist, takes into account the structural constraints conceived as 'hardware' limitations. In this sense it is a highly promising development of Piagetian theory which can account for much of the challenging data we have collected in previous chapters (e.g. that on stage heterogeneity, *horizontal décalage*, and precocious behaviours for example).

Conclusion

We wish to state again that we have not introduced an information processing approach as a panacea, for there is ample literature and lively debate to demonstrate its problems. Our aim has been simply to show that there are developments which might enable us to avoid some of the formidable obstacles of Piaget's theory.

As to the orthodox theory, we feel that there are serious problems of interpretation and validation, some of which may not be soluble. It is fitting that a theory should provide us with a step on which we can reach new levels of understanding. We feel that the time has come to take that step.

Bibliography

Allport, D. (1975), 'The state of cognitive psychology', *Quarterly Journal of Experimental Psychology*, 27, 141-52.

Ammon, P. R. (1977), 'Cognitive development and early childhood education', in H. L. Homs and P. A. Robinson (eds), *Psychological Processes in Early Education*, New York: Academic Press.

Ashton, P. T. (1975), 'Cross-cultural Piagetian research: an experimental perspective', *Harvard Educational Review*, 45, 475-506.

Blasi, A. and Hoeffel, E. C. (1974), 'Adolescence and formal operations', *Human Development*, 17, 344-63.

Bloor, D. (1977), 'The regulatory function of language: an analysis and contribution to the current controversy over the Soviet theory', in J. Morton and J. C. Marshal (eds), Psycholinguistics Series I: *Developmental and Pathological*, London: Elek.

Boonsong, S. (1968), 'The development of conservation of mass, weight and volume in Thai children', unpublished M.Ed. thesis, College of Education, Bangkok.

Borke, H. (1978), 'Piaget's view of sound interaction and the theoretical construct of empathy', in L. S. Siegel and C. J. Brainerd (eds), *Alternatives to Piaget: critical essays on the theory*, New York: Academic Press.

Bovet, M. (1974), 'Cross-cultural study of conservation concepts: continuous quantities and length', in Inhelder *et al.* (1974), *Learning and the Development of Cognition*, London: Routledge & Kegan Paul.

Bower, T. G. R. (1967), 'The development of object permanence: some studies of object constancy', *Perception and Psychophysics*, 2, 411-18.

Bower, T. G. R. (1974), *Development in Infancy*, San Francisco: Freeman.

Braine, M. D. S. (1959), 'The ontogeny of certain logical operations: Piaget's formulation examined by non-verbal methods', *Psychological Monographs*, 73 (no. 475).

Braine, M. D. S. (1964), 'The development of a grasp of transitivity of length: a reply to Smedslund', *Child Development*, 35, 799-810.

Braine, M. D. S. (1968), 'The ontogeny of certain logical operations:

Piaget's formulation examined by non-verbal methods', in I. E. Sigel and F. H. Hooper (eds), *Logical Thinking in Children*, London: Holt, Rinehart & Winston.

Brainerd, C. J. (1973a), 'Order of acquisition of transitivity, conservation and class inclusion of length and weight', *Developmental Psychology*, 8, 105-16.

Brainerd, C. J. (1973b), 'Neo-Piagetian training experiments revisited: is there any support for the cognitive-developmental stage hypothesis?', *Cognition*, 2, 349-70.

Brainerd, C. J. (1973c), 'Judgements and explanations as criteria for the presence of cognitive structures', *Psychological Bulletin*, 79, 172-9.

Brainerd, C. J. (1975), 'Structures-of-the whole and elementary education', *American Educational Research Journal*, 12, 369-78.

Brainerd, C. J. (1977a), 'Response criteria in concept development research', *Child Development*, 48, 360-6.

Brainerd, C. J. (1977b), 'Cognitive development and concept learning: an interpretive review', *Psychological Bulletin*, 84, 919-39.

Brainerd, C. J. (1978), 'Learning research and Piagetian theory', in L. S. Siegel and C. J. Brainerd (eds), *Alternatives to Piaget: critical essays on the theory*, New York: Academic Press.

Brainerd, C. J. and Allen, T. W. (1971), 'Experimental inductions of the conservation of "first order" quantitative invariants', *Psychological Bulletin*, 75, 128-44.

Brainerd, C. J. and Hooper, F. H. (1975), 'A methodological analysis of developmental studies of identity conservation and equivalence conservation', *Psychological Bulletin*, 82, 725-37.

Broadbent, D. E. (1975), 'Cognitive psychology and education', *British Journal of Educational Psychology*, 45, 162-76.

Bruner, J. S. (1959), 'Inhelder and Piaget's "The growth of logical thinking" – I – A psychologist's viewpoint', *British Journal of Psychology*, 50, 363-70.

Bryant, P. E. (1971), 'Cognitive development', *British Medical Bulletin*, 27, 200-5.

Bryant, P. E. (1974), *Perception and Understanding in Young Children*, London: Methuen.

Bryant, P. E. (1977), 'Logical inferences and development', in B. A. Geber (ed.), *Piaget and Knowing*, London: Routledge & Kegan Paul.

Bryant, P. E. and Trabasso, T. (1971), 'Transitive inferences and memory in young children', *Nature*, 232, 456-8.

Bynum, T. W., Thomas, J. A. and Weitz, L. J. (1972), 'Truth functional logic in formal operational thinking: Inhelder and Piaget's evidence', *Developmental Psychology*, 7, 129-32.

Campbell, D. and Fiske, D. (1959), 'Convergent and discriminant validation by the multi-trait-multimethod matrix', *Psychological Bulletin*, 56, 81-105.

Case, R. (1972), 'Validation of a neo-Piagetian capacity construct', *Journal of Experimental Child Psychology*, 14, 287-302.

Case, R. (1974), 'Structures and strictures: some functional limitations on the course of cognitive growth', *Cognitive Psychology*, 6, 544-73.

Case, R. (1975), 'Responsiveness to conservation training as a function of induced subjective uncertainty, M-space, and cognitive style', unpublished MS., University of California at Berkeley.

Case, R. (1976), *The Role of Motivation in the Process of Intellectual Development*, Final Report, The Spencer Foundation (cited by Pascual-Leone, 1976).

Charlesworth, W. R. (1964), 'Instigation and maintenance of curiosity behaviour as a function of surprise vs. novel and familiar stimuli', *Child Development*, 35, 1169–86.

Charlesworth, W. R. (1969), 'The role of surprise in cognitive development', in D. Elkind and J. H. Flavell (eds), *Studies in Cognitive Development*, New York: Oxford University Press.

Chomsky, N. (1972), *Language and Mind* (enlarged edition), New York: Harcourt.

Clark, E. V. (1973), 'Non-linguistic strategies and the acquisition of word meanings', *Cognitive Psychology*, 2, 161–82.

Cole, M. (1975), 'An ethnographic psychology of cognition', in R. W. Brislin *et al.* (eds), *Cross-Cultural Perspectives on Learning*, New York: Sage.

Cole, M., Gray, J., Glick, J. A. and Sharp, D. W. (1971), *The Cultural Context of Learning and Thinking*, London: Methuen.

Cole, M., John-Steiner, V., Scribner, S. and Souberman, E. (eds) (1978), *Mind in Society*, Cambridge, Mass.: Harvard University Press.

Cole, M. and Scribner, S. (1974), *Culture and Thought: A Psychological Introduction*, London: Wiley.

Cornell, E. H. (1978), 'Learning to find things: a reinterpretation of object permanence studies', in L. S. Siegel and C. J. Brainerd (eds), *Alternatives to Piaget: critical essays on the theory*, New York: Academic Press.

Danner, F. W. and Day, M. C. (1977), 'Eliciting formal operations', *Child Development*, 48, 1600–6.

Dasen, P. R. (1970), 'Cognitive development of Aborigines in Central Australia: concrete operations and perceptual activities', unpublished Ph.D. thesis, Australian National University, Canberra, 1970.

Dasen, P. R. (1972), 'Cross-cultural Piagetian research: a summary', *Journal of Cross Cultural Psychology*, 3, 23–39.

Dasen, P. R. (1976), 'Personal Communication', in S. and C. Modgil, *Piagetian Research: Compilation and Commentary*, Slough: NFER.

De Boysson-Bardies, B. and O'Regan, K. (1973), 'What children do in spite of adults' hypotheses', *Nature*, 246, 531–4.

De Lemos, M. M. (1966), 'The development of the concept of conservation in Australian Aboriginal children', unpublished Ph.D. thesis, Australian National University, Canberra, 1966.

Deregowski, J. R. and Serpell, R. (1971), 'Performance on a sorting task: a cross-cultural experiment',*International Journal of Psychology*, 6, 273–81.

Donaldson, M. (1978), *Children's Minds*, London: Fontana.

Donaldson, M. and Balfour, G. (1968), 'Less is more: a study of language comprehension in children', *British Journal of Psychology*, 59, 461–71.

Elkind, D. (1961), 'Children's discovery of the conservation of mass, weight and volume: Piaget replication study II', *Journal of Genetic Psychology*, 98, 219–27.

Elkind, D. and Flavell, J. H. (eds) (1969), *Studies in Cognitive Development: Essays in Honor of Jean Piaget*, New York: Oxford University Press.

Elkind, D. and Sameroff, A. (1970), 'Developmental psychology', *Annual Review of Psychology*, 21, 191–238.

Ennis, R. H. (1975), 'Children's ability to handle Piaget's propositional logic: a conceptual critique', *Review of Educational Research*, 45, 1–47.

Ennis, R. H. (1978), 'Conceptualisation of children's logical competence: Piaget's propositional logic and an alternative proposal', in L. S. Siegel and C. J. Brainerd (eds), *Alternatives to Piaget: critical essays on the theory*, New York: Academic Press.

Fantz, R. I. (1964), 'Pattern vision in new-born infants', *Science*, 146, 668–70.

Feyerabend, P. K. (1970), 'Against method: outline of an anarchistic theory of knowledge', in M. Radner and S. Winokur (eds), *Minnesota studies in the philosophy of science (vol. 4)*, Minnesota: University of Minnesota Press.

Flavell, J. H. (1962), 'Discussion of paper by Kessen', in W. Kessen and C. Kuhlman (eds), 'Thought in the Young Child', *Monographs of the Society for Research in Child Development*, 65–82, no. 83.

Flavell, J. H. (1963), *The Developmental Psychology of Jean Piaget*, London: Van Nostrand.

Flavell, J. H. (1971), 'Stage related properties of cognitive development', *Cognitive Psychology*, 2, 421–53.

Flavell, J. H. (1974), 'The development of inferences about others', in T. Mischel (ed.), *Understanding Other Persons*, London: Blackwell.

Flavell, J. H. and Wohlwill, J. F. (1969), 'Formal and functional aspects of cognitive development', in D. Elkind and J. H. Flavell (eds), *Studies in Cognitive Development: Essays in Honor of Jean Piaget*, New York: Oxford University Press.

Furby, L. (1971), 'A theoretical analysis of cross-cultural research in cognitive development: Piaget's conservation task', *Journal of Cross-cultural Psychology*, 2, 241–55.

Furth, H. (1977), 'The operative and figurative aspects of knowledge in Piaget's theory', in B. A. Geber (ed.), *Piaget and Knowing: Studies in Genetic Epistemology*, London: Routledge & Kegan Paul.

Gagné, R. M. (1970), *The Conditions of Learning*, London: Holt, Rinehart & Winston.

Gelman, R. (1969), 'Conservation acquisition: a problem of learning to attend to relevant attributes', *Journal of Experimental Child Psychology*, 7, 167–87.

Gelman, R. (1972), 'The nature and development of early number concepts', in H. W. Reese (ed.), *Advances in Child Development and Behaviour*, vol. 7, London: Academic Press.

Gelman, R. (1977), 'How young children reason about small numbers', in N. J. Castellan, D. B. Pisoni and G. R. Potts (eds), *Cognitive*

Theory, vol. 2, Hillsdale, New Jersey: Lawrence Erlbaum.

Gelman, R. and Tucker, M. F. (1975), 'Further investigations of the young child's conception of number', *Child Development*, 46, 167–75.

Gibson, E. J., Gibson, J. J., Pick, A. D. and Osser, H. (1962), 'A developmental study of the discrimination of letter-like forms', *Journal of Comparative Physiological Psychology*, 55, 897.

Glaser, R. and Resnick, L. B. (1972), 'Instructional psychology', in P. H. Mussen and M. Rosenzweig (eds), *Annual Review of Psychology*, Palo Alto: Annual Review.

Goodnow, J. J. (1969a), 'Problems in research on culture and thought', in D. Elkind and J. H. Flavell (eds), *Studies in Cognitive Development*, New York: Oxford University Press.

Goodnow, J. J. (1969b), 'Cultural variations in cognitive skills', in D. R. Price-Williams (ed.), *Cross-Cultural studies*, Harmondsworth: Penguin.

Goodnow, J. J. (1973), 'Compensation arguments on conservation tasks', *Developmental Psychology*, 8, 140.

Gratch, G. (1975), 'Recent studies based on Piaget's view of object concept development', in L. Cohen and P. Salapatek (eds), *Infant Perception: From Sensation to Cognition*, vol. 2, New York: Academic Press.

Gratch, G. (1976), 'On levels of awareness of objects in infants and students thereof', *Merrill-Palmer Quarterly*, 22, 157–76.

Gratch, G., Appel, K. J., Evans, W. F., Le Compte, G. K. and Wright, N. A. (1974), 'Piaget's stage IV object concept error: evidence of forgetting or object conception?', *Child Development*, 45, 71–7.

Greenfield, P. M. (1966), 'On culture and conservation', in J. S. Bruner, R. R. Olver and P. M. Greenfield (eds), *Studies in Cognitive Growth*, New York: Wiley.

Greenfield, P. M. (1969), 'On culture and conservation', in D. R. Price-Williams (ed.), *Cross-cultural Studies*, Harmondsworth: Penguin.

Greenfield, P. M. (1974), 'Comparing dimensional categorisation in natural and artificial contexts: a developmental study among the Zinacanticos of Mexico', *Journal of Social Psychology*, 93, 157–71.

Halford, G. and Galloway, W. (1977), 'Children who fail to make transitive inferences can remember comparisons', *Australian Journal of Psychology*, 29, 1, 1–5.

Hall, V. C. and Kaye, D. B. (1978), 'The necessity of logical necessity in Piaget's theory', in L. S. Siegel and C. J. Brainerd (eds), *Alternatives to Piaget: critical essays on the theory*, New York: Academic Press.

Hamel, B. R. (1974), *Children from 5–7*, Rotterdam University Press.

Harris, P. L. (1973), 'Perseveration errors in search by young children', *Child Development*, 44, 28–33.

Harris, P. L. (1974), 'Perseverative search at a visibly empty place by young infants', *Journal of Experimental Child Psychology*, 18, 535–42.

Harris, P. L. (1975), 'Inferences and semantic development', *Journal of Child Language*, 2, 143–52.

Harris, P. L. and Bassett, E. (1975), 'Transitive inferences by four year old children?', *Developmental Psychology*, 11, 875–6.

Heron, A. (1971), 'Concrete operations, "g" and achievement in Zambian children', *Journal of Cross-cultural Psychology*, 2, 325–36.

Heron, A. and Dowel, W. (1973), 'The questionable unity of the concrete operations stage', *International Journal of Psychology*, 9, 1, 1–9.

Heron, A. and Dowel, W. (1978), 'Weight conservation and matrix-solving ability in Papuan children', *Journal of Cross-Cultural Psychology*, 4, 207–19.

Hyde, D. M. (1959), 'An investigation of Piaget's theories of the development of the concept of number', unpublished Ph.D. dissertation, University of London.

Inhelder, B. (1972), 'Information processing tendencies in recent experiments in cognitive learning—empirical studies', in S. Farnham-Diggory (ed.), *Information Processing in Children*, New York: Academic Press.

Inhelder, B. and Piaget, J. (1958), *The Growth of Logical Thinking from Childhood to Adolescence*, New York: Basic Books.

Inhelder, B. and Sinclair, H. (1969), 'Learning cognitive structures', in P. H. Mussen, J. Langer and M. Covington (eds), *Trends and Issues in Developmental Psychology*, New York: Holt, Rinehart & Winston.

Inhelder, B., Sinclair, H. and Bovet, M. (1974), *Learning and the Development of Cognition*, London: Routledge & Kegan Paul.

Isaacs, N. (1951), 'Critical notice: traité de logique—essai de logistique operatoire by J. Piaget', *British Journal of Psychology*, 42, 185–8.

Jarvis, P. E. (1963), 'The effect of self-administered verbal instructions on simple sensory-motor performance in children', unpublished Ph.D. thesis, University of Rochester, New York.

Karmiloff-Smith, A. and Inhelder, B. (1975), 'If you want to get ahead, get a theory', *Cognition*, 3, 3, 195–212.

Keat, R. and Urry, J. (1975), *Social Theory as Science*, London: Routledge & Kegan Paul.

Kendler, H. H. and Kendler, T. S. (1961), 'Effects of verbalisation on reversal shifts in children', *Science*, 134, 1619–20.

Kendler, H. H. and Kendler, T. S. (1962), 'Vertical and Horizontal processes in problem solving', *Psychological Review*, 69, 1–16.

Kendler, H. H. and Kendler, T. S. (1975), 'From discrimination learning to cognitive development: a neobehavioristic odyssey', in W. K. Estes (ed.) (1975), *Handbook of learning and cognitive processes*, Hillsdale, N. Jersey: Lawrence Erlbaum.

Kingsley, R. and Hall, V. C. (1967), 'Training conservation of weight and length through learning sets', *Child Development*, 38, 1111–26.

Kitchener, R. F. (1978), 'Epigenesis: the role of biological models in developmental psychology', *Human Development*, 21, 3, 141–60.

Klahr, D. and Wallace, J. G. (1976), *Cognitive Development: An Information Processing View*, New York: Lawrence Erlbaum.

Koch, S. (ed.) (1959), *Psychology: A Study of a Science*, vol. 3, New York: McGraw Hill.

Koch, S. (1974), 'Psychology as a science', in S. C. Brown (ed.), *Philosophy of psychology*, London: Macmillan.

Kuenne, M. R. (1946), 'Experimental investigation of the relation of language to transposition behaviour in young children', *Journal of Experimental Psychology*, 36, 471–90.

Kuhn, D. (1974), 'Inducing development experimentally: comments on a research paradigm', *Developmental Psychology*, 10, 590–600.

Kuhn, T. S. (1970), *The Structure of Scientific Revolutions*, Chicago: University of Chicago Press.

Labov, W. (1970), 'The logic of non standard English', in F. Williams (ed.), *Language and Poverty*, Chicago: Markham.

Lakatos, I. and Musgrave, A. (eds) (1970), *Criticism and the Growth of Scientific Knowledge*, Cambridge: Cambridge University Press.

Lefebvre, M. and Pinard, A. (1972), 'Apprentissage de la conservation des quantités par une méthode de conflit cognitif', *Canadian Journal of Behavioral Sciences*, 4, 1–12.

Lefebvre, M. and Pinard, A. (1974), 'Influence du niveau initial de sensibilité au conflit sur l'apprentissage de la conservation des quantités par une méthode de conflit cognitif', *Canadian Journal of Behavioral Sciences*, 61, 398–413.

Lovell, K. (1961), *The Growth of Basic Mathematical and Scientific Concepts in Children*, London: University of London Press.

Luria, A. R. (1959), 'The directive function of speech in development and dissolution', *Word*, 15, 341–52 and 453–64, in R. C. Oldfield and J. C. Marshall (eds) (1968), *Language*, Harmondsworth: Penguin.

Luria, A. R. (1961), *The Role of Speech in the Regulation of Normal and Abnormal Behaviour*, New York: Liveright.

MacNamara, J. (1975), 'A note on Piaget and Number', *Child Development*, 46, 424–9.

MacNamara, J., Baker, E. and Olsen, C. L. (1976), 'Four-year-olds' understanding of pretend, forget, and know, evidence for propositional operations', *Child Development*, 47, 62–70.

Martin, L. J. (1976), 'An analysis of some of Piaget's topological tasks from a mathematical point of view', *Journal for Research in Mathematics Education*, 7, 8–24.

Martorano, S. C. (1977), 'A developmental analysis of performance on Piaget's formal operations tasks', *Developmental Psychology*, 13, 666–72.

Mehler, J. and Bever, T. G. (1967), 'Cognitive capacity of very young children', *Science*, 158, 141–2.

Miller, S. A. (1976), 'Non verbal assessment of Piagetian concepts', *Psychological Bulletin*, 83, 3, 405–30.

Miller, S., Shelton, J. and Flavell, J. (1970), 'A test of Luria's hypothesis concerning the development of verbal self-regulation', *Child Development*, 41, 651–65.

Milner, P. M. (1970), *Physiological Psychology*, New York: Holt, Rinehart & Winston.

Modgil, S. (1974), *Piagetian Research, A Handbook of Recent Studies*, Slough: NFER.

Modgil, S. and Modgil, C. (1976), *Piagetian Research: Compilation and Commentary*, Slough: NFER.

Mohseni, N. (1966), *La comparaison des reactions aux épreuves d'intelligence en Iran et en Europe*, Thèse de l'université, University of Paris, 1966.

Murray, F. B., Ames, G. J. and Botvin, G. J. (1977), 'Acquisition of conservation through cognitive dissonance', *Journal of Educational Psychology*, 69, 5, 519–27.

Murray, J. P. and Youniss, J. (1968), 'Achievement of inferential transitivity and its relation to serial ordering', *Child Development*, 39, 1259–68.

Neimark, E. D. (1975), 'Longitudinal development of formal operations thought', *Genetic Psychology Monographs*, 91, 171–225.

Neisser, U. (1967), *Cognitive Psychology*, New York: Appleton-Century-Crofts.

Newell, A. (1974), 'You can't play 20 questions with nature and win', in W. G. Chase (ed.), *Visual Information Processing*, New York: Academic Press.

Odom, R. D. (1978), 'A perceptual salience account of décalage relations and development change', in L. S. Siegel and C. J. Brainerd (eds), *Alternatives to Piaget: critical essays on the theory*, New York: Academic Press.

Okonji, M. O. (1971), 'Culture and children's understanding of geometry', *British Journal of Psychology*, 6, 121–8.

Osgood, C. E. (1957), 'A behavioristic analysis of perception, and language as cognitive phenomena', *Contemporary Approaches to Cognition: University of Colorado Symposium*, Cambridge, Mass.: Harvard University Press.

Papalia, D. E. and Hooper, F. H. (1971), 'A developmental comparison of identity and equivalence conservation', *Journal of Experimental Child Psychology*, 12, 347–61.

Parkinson, G. M. (1969), 'The recognition of messages from visual compound stimuli: a test of a quantitative developmental model', unpublished M.A. thesis, York University.

Parsons, C. (1960), 'Inhelder and Piaget's "The Growth of logical thinking": II A logician's viewpoint', *British Journal of Psychology*, 51, 75–84.

Pascual-Leone, J. (1970), 'A mathematical model for the transition rule in Piaget's developmental stages', *Acta Psychologica*, 32, 301–45.

Pascual-Leone, J. (1976), 'On learning and development, Piagetian style: 1. A reply to Lefebvre-Pinard', *Canadian Psychological Review*, 17, 4, 270–84.

Phillips, D. C. and Kelly, M. E. (1975), 'Hierarchical theories of development in Education and Psychology', *Harvard Educational Review*, 45, 3, 351–75.

Piaget, J. (1926), *The Language and Thought of the Child* (revised 1959), London: Routledge & Kegan Paul.

Piaget, J. (1929), *The Child's Conception of the World*, London: Routledge & Kegan Paul.

Piaget, J. (1942), *Classes, relations et nombres; essai sur le 'groupement' de la logistique et la reversibilité de la pensée*, Paris: Vrin.

Piaget, J. (1949), *Traité de logique*, Paris: Colin.

Piaget, J. (1950), *The Psychology of Intelligence*, London: Routledge & Kegan Paul.

Piaget, J. (1952), *The Child's Conception of Number*, London: Routledge & Kegan Paul.

Piaget, J. (1953), 'How children form mathematical concepts', *Scientific American*, November.

Piaget, J. (1955), *The Child's Construction of Reality*, London: Routledge & Kegan Paul.

Piaget, J. (1957a), 'Logique et équilibre dans les comportements du sujet', in L. Apostel, B. Mandelbrot, and J. Piaget (eds), *Logique et équilibre*. *Etudes d'epistémologie génétique*, vol. 2, Paris: Presses Universitaire de France, 1957.

Piaget, J. (1957b), *Logic and Psychology*, New York: Basic Books.

Piaget, J. (1962), 'The stages of the intellectual development of the child', reprinted in P. C. Wason and P. N. Johnson-Laird (eds), *Thinking and Reasoning*, Harmondsworth: Penguin.

Piaget, J. (1967), *Six Psychological Studies*, New York: Random House.

Piaget, J. (1970a), *Science of Education and the Psychology of the Child*, London: Longman.

Piaget, J. (1970b), 'Piaget's theory', in J. Mussen (ed.), *Carmichael's Manual of Child Psychology*, 3rd edn vol. 1, New York: Wiley.

Piaget, J. (1970c), *Genetic Epistemology*, New York: Columbia University Press.

Piaget, J. (1971a), *Structuralism*, London: Routledge & Kegan Paul.

Piaget, J. (1971b), *Biology and Knowledge*, Chicago: University of Chicago Press.

Piaget, J. (1972a), 'Intellectual evolution from adolescence to adulthood', *Human Development*, 15, 1-12.

Piaget, J. (1972b), *The Principles of Genetic Epistemology*, London: Routledge & Kegan Paul.

Piaget, J. (1976), 'Need and significance of cross-cultural studies in genetic psychology', in B. Inhelder and H. H. Chipman (eds), *Piaget and his School*, New York: Springer Verlag, 1976.

Piaget, J. (1978), *The Development of Thought: Equilibration of Cognitive Structures*, London: Blackwell.

Piaget, J. and Inhelder, B. (1956), *The Child's Conception of Space*, London: Routledge & Kegan Paul.

Piaget, J. and Inhelder, B. (1964), *The Early Growth of Logic in the Child. Classification and Seriation*, London: Routledge & Kegan Paul.

Piaget, J. and Inhelder, B. (1967), *The Child's Conception of Space*, London: Routledge & Kegan Paul.

Piaget, J. and Inhelder, B. (1969), *The Psychology of the Child*, London: Routledge & Kegan Paul.

Piaget, J., Inhelder, B. and Szeminska, A. (1960), *A Child's Conception of Geometry*, London: Routledge & Kegan Paul.

Piaget, J. and Szeminska, A. (1952), *The Child's Conception of Number*, London: Routledge & Kegan Paul.

Pinard, A. and Laurendeau, M. (1969), ' "Stage" in Piaget's cognitive-developmental theory: exegesis of a concept', in D. Elkind and J. H. Flavell (eds), *Studies in Cognitive Development: Essays in Honor of Jean Piaget*, New York: Oxford University Press.

Povey, R. M. and Hill, E. (1975), 'Can pre-school children form concepts?', *Educational Research*, 17, 180-92.

Price-Williams, D. R. (1961), 'A study concerning concepts of conservation of quantities among primitive children', *Acta Psychologica*, 18, 297–305.

Price-Williams, D. R. (ed) (1969), *Cross-cultural studies*, Harmondsworth: Penguin.

Price-Williams, D. R., Gordon, W. and Ramirez (1969), 'Skill and conservation: a study of pottery-making children', *Developmental Psychology*, 1, 769.

Prince, J. R. (1968), 'Science concepts in New Guinean and European children', *Australian Journal of Education*, 12, 81–9.

Riley, C. A. and Trabasso, T. (1974), 'Comparatives, logical structures and encoding in a transitive inference task', *Journal of Experimental Child Psychology*, 17, 187–203.

Roodin, M. L. and Gruen, G. E. (1970), 'The role of memory in making transitive judgements', *Journal of Experimental Child Psychology*, 10, 264–75.

Rose, S. A. and Blank, M. (1974), 'The potency of context in children's cognition: an illustration through conservation', *Child Development*, 45, 499–502.

Rowell, J. A. and Renner, V. J. (1976), 'Quantity conceptions in university students: another look', *British Journal of Psychology*, 67, 1–10.

Sahakian, W. S. (1975), *History and Systems of Psychology*, New York: Wiley.

Scardamalia, M. (1977), 'Information processing capacity and the problem of horizontal décalage: a demonstration using combinatorial reasoning tasks', *Child Development*, 48, 28–37.

Schwebel, M. (1975), 'Formal operations in first year college students', *Journal of Psychology*, 91, 133–41.

Sheppard, J. L. (1974), 'Compensation and combinatorial systems in the acquisition and generalisation of conservation', *Child Development*, 45, 717–30.

Siegel, L. S. (1978), 'The relationship of language and thought in the preoperational child: a reconsideration of nonverbal alternatives to Piagetian tasks', in L. S. Siegel and C. J. Brainerd (eds), *Alternatives to Piaget: Critical Essays on the Theory*, New York: Academic Press.

Siegel, L. S. and Brainerd, C. J. (eds) (1978), *Alternatives to Piaget: Critical Essays on the Theory*, New York: Academic Press.

Sigel, I. E. and Hooper, F. H. (eds) (1968), *Logical Thinking in Children*, New York: Holt, Rinehart & Winston.

Sinclair, H. (1969), 'Developmental psycholinguistics', in D. Elkind and J. H. Flavell (eds), *Studies in Cognitive Development*, New York: Oxford University Press.

Smedslund, J. (1961a), 'The acquisition of conservation of substance and weight in children. II External reinforcement of conservation of weight and the operations of addition and subtraction', *Scandinavian Journal of Psychology*, 2, 71–84.

Smedslund, J. (1961b), 'The acquisition of conservation of substance and weight in children. IV. An attempt at extinction of the visual components of the weight concept', *Scandinavian Journal of Psychology*, 2, 153–5.

Smedslund, J. (1963), 'Development of concrete transitivity of length in children', *Child Development*, 34, 389–405.

Smedslund, J. (1965), 'The development of transitivity of length: a comment on Braine's reply', *Child Development*, 36, 577–80.

Smedslund, J. (1977), 'Piaget's psychology in practice', *British Journal of Educational Psychology*, 47, 1–6.

Strauss, S. (1972), 'Inducing cognitive development and learning: a review of short-term training experiments. 1. The organismic developmental approach', *Cognition*, 1, 329–57.

Towler, J. O. and Wheatley, G. (1971), 'Conservation concepts in college students: a replication and critique', *Journal of Genetic Psychology*, 118, 265–70.

Trabasso, T. (1975), 'Representation, memory and reasoning; How do we make transitive inferences?', in A. D. Pick (ed.), *Minnesota symposium on child psychology*, vol. 9, Minneapolis: University of Minneapolis Press.

Trabasso, T. (1977), 'The role of memory as a system in making transitive inferences', in R. V. Kail and J. W. Hagen (eds), *Perspectives on the Development of Memory and Cognition*, Hillsdale, N.J.: Lawrence Erlbaum.

Uzgiris, I. (1962), 'On the situational generality of conservation', unpublished Ph.D. dissertation, University of Illinois.

Vernon, P. E. (1976), 'Environment and intelligence', in P. Varma and P. Williams (eds), *Piaget: Psychology and Education*, London: Hodder and Stoughton.

Vygotsky, L. S. (1962), *Thought and Language*, Cambridge, Mass.: MIT Press.

Wallace, J. G. (1976), 'The course of cognitive growth', in V. P. Varma and P. Williams (eds), *Piaget, Psychology and Education*, London: Hodder and Stoughton.

Wallace, J. G. (1978), 'Cognitive development', in D. Fontana (ed.), *The Education of the Young Child*, London: Open Books.

Wason, P. C. and Johnson-Laird, P. N. (1972), *Psychology of Reasoning: Structure and Content*, London: Batsford.

Wilder, L. (1968), 'The role of speech and other extra-signal feedback in the regulation of the child's sensory motor behaviour', *Speech Monographs*, 423–34.

Youniss, J. and Furth, H. G. (1973), 'Reasoning and Piaget', *Nature*, of children's inference', *Child Development*, 42, 1837–47.

Younniss, J. and Furth, H. G. (1973), 'Reasoning and Piaget', *Nature*, 244, 314–15.

Za'rour, G. I. (1971), 'Conservation of weight across different materials by Lebanese school children in Beirut', *Science Education*, 35, 387–94.

Zimmerman, B. J. and Rosenthal, T. L. (1974), 'Observational learning of rule-governed behaviour by children', *Psychological Bulletin*, 81, 29–42.

Index

30, 330